YOU TURN

For When the Nearest Exit is Behind You

Kevin A. Thompson

Forte Media Publishing
Fort Smith, Arkansas

You Turn

©2015 by Kevin A. Thompson

Published by: Forte Media Publishing
Designed by Kerry Ward

ISBN: 978-0692572399

Printed in the United States of America

To four women,

The first to read to me, my mom.

*The two who taught me to write,
Mrs. Kaundart and Mrs. Colyer.*

*And the one for whom no words
adequately describe my love, Jenny.*

Table of Contents

Table of Contents

Table of Contents

Introduction

60 seconds. That's how long you have before the smoke overtakes the cabin and renders you helpless. As the plane was gathering speed something went wrong. The skilled pilot was able to abort the takeoff. Before even being fully stopped, the flight attendants begin telling you to exit the plane. In one minute the smoke will overtake the cabin. The choices you make will be the difference between life and death.

15 rows ahead of you is an exit. 96 people stand between you and safety. Will you live or die?

The difference between the two is most likely found in whether or not you remember the most obvious piece of information—that the nearest exit may be behind you.

With one turn of your head, you could see an exit two rows behind you with only 6 people between you and safety. Go backwards and you surely live. Go forward and the chances of living are a coin toss.

Airline safety experts are keenly aware of a deep flaw within humanity. In times of stress, we often forget the most obvious information. As the plane pushes back from the jetway, everyone knows emergency exits are in front of them and behind them. Yet add stress to the equation and our chances of remembering that simple fact is greatly decreased.

To assist us, the FAA mandates the airlines remind us of this fact on every flight. The information is so obvious, few passengers pay attention. But for those that do and take the time to turn their head to identify their nearest exit, their chances of surviving a crash are much higher.

What's true of airplanes is often true of life. Every day our lives are destroyed because we forget obvious information. At work, in relationships, during grief, and in other stressful times of life, our judgment is clouded. We forget relevant facts and we do what comes most naturally. Unfortunately, our natural responses are not always the right responses.

We need help.

Airlines know there are two ways to assist passengers in times of trouble. During an emergency, crew members can point passengers in the right direction. For those who can hear and see the instructions, this is a very effective form of communication. Passengers need help and the flight attendants know what to do.

However, with only a few flight attendants and many passengers, only a few can be saved by this method. The way to help everyone is to give the relevant information before a tragedy occurs. So the FAA requires each airline to remind passengers of important information before every flight. Those that pay attention and plan are far more likely to survive in the case of an accident. The problem is that many people do not listen to these announcements because they think the information is obvious.

You Turn is both a preparation before, and reminder during, the stressful times of life. It points us to the better ways which are often forgotten or unseen.

For some, it is like a pre-flight announcement. Much of the information is obvious. Without a specific circumstance in mind, principles can be learned and stored for a later time. If this is you, start reading chapter one and read it like any other book.

For others, the cabin is already on fire. We need help because we've done what seems most obvious and it's not working. This book will be like a well-positioned flight attendant who can see the panic in our eyes. It will remind us of some simple truths which we need to follow in order to live. If this is you, find the most relevant chapter and dig in.

Notice the title is *You Turn*.

Too many people are waiting. They are waiting on a boss or a job or a break or a friend or a spouse. They are waiting on someone or something to change their life. But others can't change you. They can help, support, love, and assist. *You Turn* is about the control we have over our own lives. We don't control everything, but we do control many of the important things.

As a pastor, I often interact with people on their worst days. While every situation is unique, many common themes can be found. Some areas in life are more difficult than others—fear, mistakes, relationships, work, and grief often become stumbling blocks for people. Because we focus on the wrong things, ignore our responsibilities, and make bad decisions we often struggle with aspects of life.

You Turn gives us an emergency plan for the stressful areas of life.

Stop making excuses, tell yourself the truth, and find a better way.

"Stop making excuses, tell yourself the truth, and find a better way."

Notes

1

Focus

Events come in waves. A few months ago I visited three different couples in the hospital, each of whom had delivered a baby. Two weeks ago three affairs were exposed in one morning. This week has been a week of funerals.

While death is a constant aspect of life, I've been struck by one idea as I have attended or performed funerals—this life matters.

It's easy to get caught up in day-to-day living and be deceived into thinking that our lives do not really matter. The world existed before we got here and it will keep going after we are gone. If we aren't careful, we can believe our decisions really don't have an impact.

Yet our lives do matter.

Having buried good people (and some not so good people), having sat with parents as they grieved the loss of a child, having stood beside the casket with many a son or daughter wondering if the deceased parent loved them or cared, having wrestled through the difficult choices of life with many a person, I can verify that what we do does matter.

It matters what we do. Our actions have lasting consequences for ourselves and others. We might like to think we're different, but bad decisions hurt. Good decisions can have lasting consequences we can't even begin to imagine. Our actions count. For better or worse, what we do has a tremendous impact on others. We should never take our actions lightly.

It matters what we say. When I was notified of a tragic death this week, my first thoughts were of the last conversation I had with the person. It was a meaningful talk in which the person truly revealed their heart. What a blessing it is to have that memory of this friend. He spoke his heart and for that I am grateful. Yet it's not just last words that matter. I can think back to many conversations from the past—both good and bad—that are still with me. Even if the person is gone, their words continue to influence my life.

It matters what we believe. Beliefs have consequences. Every belief cannot be the same; they cannot be equal. There is a right and wrong. What we believe matters. It influences our decision making, our priorities, and our lives. What we do is born in our belief systems. Those beliefs matter too much to be left to chance or ignored. We must take the time to consider the truth, find it, and live by it.

Every time I stand behind a casket and give a eulogy, I am reminded that I could be just 48 hours away from either being in the casket or sitting on the front row for the funeral service of any one of my friends or loved ones.

The prophet says we are but "a step from death."

While we live in daily denial of this truth—in part, to preserve our

Every time I stand behind a casket and give a eulogy, I am reminded that I could be just 48 hours away from either being in the casket or sitting on the front row for the funeral service of any one of my friends or loved ones.

own sanity—we would do well to occasionally remind ourselves of that reality. We won't be here forever. At any moment, we could meet our end. And at that moment, everything we have done, said, and believed will matter more than we understand.

If you died right now:

- What would be your legacy?

- What would be the lasting words your kids or spouse would remember?

- What issues would be left unresolved for those you love?

- What questions would they have that you have left unanswered?

- Would they know you loved them?

- Would they be at peace regarding your relationship with them? With others? With God?

- If you are unhappy with any of your answers, change that today.

- Trust me, it matters.

Love + Knowledge = What Is Best

From the moment I saw my first equation in math class, I wondered what this had to do with real life? The teacher reassured us, "You will spend the rest of your life figuring out equations." And she was right.

On a daily basis, I'm working equations:

- Do flowers plus a clean kitchen equal a happy wife?
- Does a rerun of *Full House* and a bowl full of goldfish crackers equal quiet children?
- Does a busy week and completed chores equal the freedom to play golf Saturday morning?

From the moment we learn 1+1=2, we spend the rest of our lives trying to solve the difficult equations of life.

What equals a:

- happy marriage
- healthy kids
- sufficient retirement

When it comes to figuring out the best action we should take, there is a simple equation:

Love + Knowledge = What Is Best

The most common mistake regarding this equation is assuming that either love or knowledge will lead to the best action. People often believe it is one or the other.

Some believe all we need is love. They think if their desire is right, their actions will follow. While love is important, love alone does not lead to what is best. Love creates action. It motivates us to move. It propels us into motion. Yet it doesn't tell us what we should do. Love does not necessarily drive us in the right direction. It might create action, but it doesn't ensure the right action. How many evils have been done in the name of love? How many foolish actions have resulted because of foolish love? How well do we know that it is often better to do nothing than the wrong thing? Love without knowledge does not lead to what is best.

Some believe all we need is knowledge. They think if their ideas are right, their actions will follow. While knowledge is important, knowledge alone does not lead to what is best. Knowledge rarely leads to action. It might show us the way to go, but it rarely causes us to go that way. Knowledge rarely motivates. Does knowing the truth cause us to eat properly? Does awareness of the facts motivate us to exercise? Do the right ideas always lead to the best outcomes? Knowledge without love does not lead to what is best.

We need both—love and knowledge.
Without love, knowledge rarely moves.
Without knowledge, love rarely moves
in the right direction.

Love + Knowledge = What Is Best

Whenever we are considering what action to take, we must check both aspects.

Rarely do we have all the knowledge we need to make a good choice. We need to seek wise advisors, read books, and learn new skills.

Rarely do we have all the love we need to make a good choice. We need to check our hearts, be reminded of the true nature of love, and put the needs of others before ourselves.

If you want to make the best choice possible, realize what stands between you and wisdom. Seek love and knowledge and what is best will likely follow.

"If you want to make the best choice possible, realize what stands between you and wisdom. Seek love and knowledge, then what is best will likely follow."

I don't run.

I don't refuse a steak when offered.

I don't get up at 4am, put on camouflage and cover myself in deer urine.

Why? Because I'm not a runner, a vegetarian, or a hunter. Because I am not those things, there are certain things I do not do.

Years ago, I would not carry a pink backpack and play with dolls, but all of that changed when I became a father of a little girl. Now, it's not unusual for me to have a pink coat in one hand, a pink backpack in the other, and be discussing the latest quandary of a *Max and Ruby* cartoon. I do these things because I am a father.

One of the greatest questions people struggle to answer is, "What should I do?" From the junior high student making their class schedule to the college student soon to graduate to the stressed out new mom running a house and a career, "What should I do?" is one of the preeminent questions in every aspect of life.

From the big questions of life:

- What job should I take?
- In what city should I make my home?
- What sort of person should I marry?

to the everyday issues of life:

- What should be my response to this offense?
- What should be my reaction to this request?
- What should be my decision on this problem?

The question of "what" haunts each of us on a daily basis.

As a parent, I spend most of my time telling my children what they should and shouldn't do.

As a leader, I spend a majority of my time asking my co-workers what they are doing about certain issues.

As a citizen, I spend my energy focusing on what the government is or is not doing.

Life is most often defined by the "whats."

- What should I do with my life?
- What should I do with this opportunity?
- What should I do with this person?
- What should I do with this time?

Life is lived in the "whats," yet the "whats" of life should never be answered in isolation.

The "whats" of life must always be answered in the context of the "who" of life.

Who am I? And more important: Who do I want to be?

The Who should always precede the What.

Until we decide who we are and who we want to be, we can never fully answer what we should do in any given situation.

Why does a person struggle to lose weight? When it comes time to decide what to eat, they don't make that decision based on who they want to be.

Why do marriages fail? Couples are making thousands of small decisions without considering who they want to be.

Why do companies, churches, and communities drift from their original mission? They lose sight of who they want to be.

Many people struggle with the "what" questions, because they have never taken time to consider who they want to become. With no defining vision, it is nearly impossible to determine what action to take.

Yet when the "who" is defined, the "whats" become easier.

What I should do always flows from who I want to be. Define the "who" and the "whats" will follow.

We had a breakdown last night.

My son was doing something irritating. I told him to stop. When he didn't, I warned him that one more act would get his Christmas present placed in timeout. He acted and so did I.

He went crazy—like a five–year-old this-would-never-happen-in-front-of-anyone-but-his-parents crazy.

It was so over the top, I took him upstairs, turned off the lights, and held him down while rocking in the rocking chair.

Eventually he calmed down enough so that I could ask him questions.

He explained why he was mad and why he threw his fit.

I asked, "What did you think the yelling, screaming, and kicking would get you?"

He said, "I thought it would cause you to give me my toy back."

I nearly laughed out loud. "So you thought that by acting horribly, I would give your toy back?"

He said, "Yes."

I then explained what I have explained a thousand times before: good choices lead to good consequences and bad choices lead to bad consequences. I assured him I would never reward the behavior he was exhibiting by giving him what he wanted.

He seemed to understand. In an unusual moment, he calmed down, apologized, and we returned downstairs.

He got it.
I wish we would.

When things do not go our way, we often respond the way we feel

"When things do not go our way, we often respond the way we feel with the hopes that our response will get us what we want.

What we fail to realize is that what we are doing will rarely result in what we desire and might actually be preventing the outcome we want."

with the hopes that our response will get us what we want.

What we fail to realize is that what we are doing will rarely result in what we desire and might actually be preventing the outcome we want.

Several years ago a mom came to see me. She was angry over her son's playing time and was on her way to see the coach. She felt her son had been treated unfairly and she was furious. I asked her what she was planning to do and she described her plan.

After listening, I asked, "What do you want the outcome of this meeting to be?"

She said, "For my son to be treated fairly and to play."

I asked, "Do you think doing what you are planning to do will result in what you want?"

Having heard it out loud, she said, "No."

We then discussed what she could do that might result in what she wanted.

In most situations, we have two choices:

1. **To do what we have a right to do.**
2. **To do what is most likely to get the result we want.**

There is a radical difference between these two choices.

Almost without fail, we foolishly choose the first option.

The good news: our actions often feel justified; we feel in the right; the other person is clearly wrong.

The bad news: our actions rarely result in the desired outcome.

The reason is obvious.

Silas learned a great lesson last night. He will spend the rest of his life re-learning it.

The question is when will we understand what even a five–year-old knows?

Is there an area where you aren't getting what you want?

Could it be that what you are doing would never result in what you want?

In most situations we have two choices:

1. To do what we have a right to do.
2. To do what is most likely to get the result we want.

There is a radical difference between these two choices.

Almost without fail, we foolishly choose the first option.

It's one of the most basic questions in life.

It's the question every salesperson is thinking as a potential customer enters the store.

It's what every parent is asking when a child pulls on their leg.

It should be the question all of us are asking as we look at ourselves in the mirror.

What do you want?

We live in a fascinating time in which the question can actually be asked. Many older generations never had the freedom to ask. They were too worried about survival, shelter, or food to ever consider the possibility of designing a life they enjoyed.

Many of us have that freedom.

We live in a fortunate day where freedom of choice abounds.

Our parents do not dictate whom we marry; we do. We aren't forever stuck in one job or career. Resources are often available, no matter one's age, to go back to school and learn new skills. We are not limited by geography. We have more opportunity than any generation before us.

Never has a group of people had the ability to pursue what they really desired as this generation. Yet rarely do individuals ask the important question—what do you want?

It is a simple question, but it is not an easy question to answer. When pressed, most people throw out an answer which is neither specific nor accurate.

They claim they want money or fame or happiness, but they can't tell you why they want money or fame, and they can't describe what happiness means for them.

Money is not what you want. We all want some of the things money can do for us, but money alone should never be the goal.

Success is what you want, but it must be defined. It can be

"Money is not what you want. We all want some of the things money can do for us, but money alone should never be the goal.

Success is what you want, but it must be defined. It can be radically different things for different people. As long as we are chasing undefined success, we will never experience success, or even if we do, we won't realize we have found it."

radically different things for different people. As long as we are chasing undefined success, we will never experience success, or even if we do, we won't realize we have found it.

There are primarily three reasons people do not define what they want:

1. **We are afraid to do the work.** Determining what we really want might be simple, but it is not easy. It takes soul-searching. It requires difficult decisions. It forces us to make a choice of what we truly value. Without the pressure of a deadline, decisions like this are easy to push until tomorrow and then the next week or next year. Decades can pass and people can realize they have never truly defined what they desire. If the question is ignored for long enough, we can lose any sense of even knowing what we want. Answering this question takes time, energy, and courage. Many people are not willing to make the sacrifices necessary to do the work.

2. **We are afraid to fail.** The scary thing about defining what you want is that you may not get it. Some people prefer to drift in ambiguity where they never have to admit they are failing rather than pursue after a goal which might result in failure. Fear paralyzes. It scares us into believing it is better to have the appearance of success than to dare experience the possibility of failure. It's a fool's trade.

3. **We have never considered the question.** Most people never define what they want simply because they have never considered the question. They've never had a mentor ask them. They've never understood the opportunity they have to define their life and their goals. Ignorance of opportunity robs many people from living the life they desire.

It's sad to consider how many people are not satisfied with life, yet they aren't asking the key questions which could lead to satisfaction. They are hopelessly drifting without any sense of control over their lives, never realizing they have the ability to make life-changing choices.

In business, marriage, parenting, and our personal lives, one of the most important questions we can ask is, "What do I want?"

When we define our desire, we have a real chance of achieving it.

Whenever I speak to someone who is just getting started in life, I often tell them what I think is the secret to a satisfying life.

Those who have a deep appreciation for life all seem to share three things in common.

These three characteristics aren't laws which are true for every person, but they are general principles that I have seen play out in the lives of hundreds of church members, friends, and those who have shared their lives with me.

If someone is seeking a satisfying life, I encourage them to locate three loves.

The Three Loves

Love what you do. Never has there been a time in which people have as much choice regarding what they do. Gone are the days of one job worked over one lifetime with the sole purpose of putting food on the table. We live in a time when people have great freedom not only to find a job that pays well, but also one they truly enjoy.

No one has to start in a job they love, but as soon as you can begin working toward that, the better off you will be. And even if you can't find a job you love, what you do does not have to be defined by your work. Maybe the job just pays the bills, but it allows you to do what you love after work and on the weekends.

Find the intersection of your passions, abilities, and the needs of the world to find something you love to do.

Love where you are. Happy people love where they live. It doesn't mean they find it perfect. As a matter of fact, the imperfection is often the key to happiness because the imperfection allows them to contribute to their community. If you are looking for the perfect place to live, you are likely to find a place that doesn't need you. Don't find a place that is perfect, find a place that is in need of what you have to offer.

Love who you're with. Life is only meaningful when shared with others. This might begin with a spouse, but it also includes friends, co-workers, and neighbors.

When I was a senior in college and was looking for the right graduate school, I sought advice from our college president. We spoke at length about which school and program might be the right one. As the conversation came to a close, he looked at me and said, "You know this really doesn't matter, right?" I was confused and asked what he meant. He said, "All your choices are good and you are making sure you make a wise decision. But where you go to school doesn't matter in comparison to who you marry. She can make you or break you." He was right.

Nothing is more influential than whom you marry, yet other relationships are vital as well. Who will you work with or for? With whom will you choose to spend your time away from work? Who will be the people in your life?

Life is much more satisfying when you spend most of your day with people you love.

A Secret About Love...

What many people fail to understand about these three pathways to happiness is that we are not enslaved to our hearts. We control our hearts far more than our hearts control us. We can choose what and whom to love.

This means if you married the wrong person, chose the wrong career, and can't stand where you live, you can change your attitude oftentimes easier than you can actually change all three. In most cases, you can learn (or re-learn) to love who you married. You can find appreciation in the job you currently have. And you can grow your passion for your current location.

While it's easier to choose the three and stay in love with them, we can also backdoor the process by learning to love our current station in life.

A Personal Note...

Few things make me feel as fortunate as the fact that I love what I do, where I do it, and with whom who I do it.

As a pastor and writer, I get to continually talk about the things I find important. While it has its challenges, it has far more joys.

I do so in the town where I was raised. It's not a perfect place, but it is a good place with good people.

And I do it in partnership with the best woman I know, working alongside my closest friends, and serving with some of the most loving people in the world.

Do you want to change your life? Learn to love what you do, where you are, and who you are with.

Nothing is more influential than whom you marry, yet other relationships are vital as well. Who will you work with or for? With whom will you choose to spend your time away from work? Who will be the people in your life?

Life is much more satisfying when you spend most of your day with people you love.

"I don't know what to do."

It's the reason a majority of people communicate with me about a situation in their life:

- A wife's heart is dying but her husband refuses to listen to her cries for help
- A student will soon graduate but few job offers are on the table
- A friendship is strained and neither friend is certain how to reconcile

Few people sit down with me with great confidence about their next step. They call because they're uncertain.

And we almost always find the next step.

We may not be able to define everything that needs to take place, but it is rarely difficult to find the next step.

"I don't know what to do," is a phrase I tell myself on many occasions.

It feels so true. A situation seems complex. Differing decisions all seem to have negative consequences. I want something to change but I don't know what to do about it.

Why is it that I so often find myself in situations where I don't know what to do, but I rarely talk to others when their next step isn't obvious?

I often don't know what I should do but rarely do I not know what others should do.

Recently, I was thinking about a situation and I began to tell myself, "I don't know what to do." The situation really perplexed me. While trying to find a solution, I tried to remember if I had ever walked beside another person as they dealt with a similar issue.

What questions did I ask? What advice did I give?

I began to realize I knew exactly what to do. I might not know all the steps I should take, but the first one or two were obvious.

While I told myself I didn't know what to do, it simply wasn't true. I knew exactly what to do, but I didn't want to do it.

I realized that's almost always the case. Nearly every time I say, "I don't know what to do," what I actually mean is, "I don't want to do what I know I should."

While there are times we do not know what to do, those times are rare. We almost always know the next step. We may not know the next ten steps. **We may not know what the outcome of the situation will be.** But rarely are we completely clueless as to what to do next.

There is a difference between not knowing what to do and not wanting to do what we know we should. The former is ignorance, the latter is cowardice. **We are cowards far more often than we are ignorant.**

Consider a situation in your life where you think you don't know what you should do. Is it true? Are you really stumped or are you rebelling against what should be done?

Notes

2

Responsibility

Foolishly unhappy. **If given just two words to describe a majority of people, these would be the two I would choose. It doesn't define everyone, but it properly describes a good number.**

Few would doubt the "unhappy" description.

A significant number of people are unhappy:

In relationships. Much is said about a high divorce rate, but many relationships are breaking before vows are even said. Fearing that marriage is insignificant or even a threat to love, many are avoiding the altar. Sadly, this avoidance is neither leading to longer relationships nor providing a more meaningful love. By skipping marriage, many are giving up on any chance of finding a lasting, significant relationship. The result is deep unhappiness.

At work. Do you know how rare it is to find someone truly satisfied with what they do on a daily basis? Clearly, no one will be happy every day at work, but it doesn't seem far-fetched to assume a general happiness on a regular basis. We spend the majority of our waking hours at work. Besides the home, if there is anywhere we seek happiness, it is at work. Yet many are frustrated, burned out, dissatisfied with their bosses, estranged from their co-workers, and unfulfilled by what they do on an average day at work.

With themselves. We all have struggles, imperfections, and character flaws. But why is it so rare to find someone who is truly happy with themselves? Even those who suffer from arrogance seem to do so as a mask to cover up their weaknesses and insecurities. Few people I know have a balanced understanding of themselves which results in a general satisfaction with whom they are.

Many are unhappy, but notice how we live. There has never been a time when an individual controls so much of their own lives. We decide whom we marry (as long as the other person says yes),

"We spend the majority of our waking hours at work. Besides the home, if there is anywhere we seek happiness, it is at work. Yet many are frustrated, burned out, dissatisfied with their bosses, estranged from their co-workers, and unfulfilled by what they do on an average day at work."

where we work (at least where we don't work), and a plethora of other aspects of our lives which many people in the past did not decide.

We control more of our lives, yet we are more unhappy than nearly any generation before us.

We are unhappy, but the source of that unhappiness is our own foolishness.

Clearly, there are exceptions. Some people have been dealt a hand in the game of life that is nearly unplayable. Their unhappiness is not their fault; it's not within their control. Yet for most of us, our satisfaction with life is 100% within our control. We have decided how to live and it has resulted in unhappiness.

Our foolishness is often sourced in three areas:

1. **A fixation on the future or past at the expense of the present:** We often spend so much time thinking about what we hope happens or remembering what we think did happen that we lose all sense of enjoyment of the present. Like a small child who desperately wants to grow up, thinking grown-ups have all the fun, many people spend their entire lives looking ahead, until one day they begin looking behind them, but at no point do they appreciate the moment. Generally, we have very little to fear or dread in the present. We often have everything we need to enjoy the next moment, but sadly we often look past the next moment, dreaming of what is to come or what once was.

2. **A deep sense of entitlement:** Many people believe they deserve happiness, as though it is a birthright. They think they should be given happiness and then they might be expected to work or make wise choices. Our sense of entitlement is so deep, we often do not see it. We actually believe we are entitled to be entitled. Believing we deserve every accolade, title, promotion, award, and recognition, robs us of one of life's greatest producers of happiness–gratitude. Without feeling gratitude, we cannot feel happy.

3. **A complete unwillingness to choose wisely:** We choose what we want, not what is best. We are often so selfishly driven

that we reject wise voices in our lives and simply pick what we desire the most. The problem is that our desires are rarely satisfied by what we think will satisfy them. We reject wisdom but then wonder why we are unhappy.

Foolishly unhappy does not describe every person I know, but it describes many. While a few lack happiness because of situations they do not control, many have chosen their unhappiness.

Yet, sadly, they do not realize they have decided their own fate.

Living in the deception that their life is out of their control, they will continue to focus on the past or future wondering why they haven't been given everything they deserve. They will reject wise choices in order to get what they want in the moment.

But it doesn't have to be that way.

We can:

Come to peace with our past, not overly worry about or long for the future, and deeply appreciate the present.

Live in a constant state of gratitude for the good we do not deserve.

Make wise choices.

This will not guarantee an unending happiness, but it will save us from the most common cause of unhappiness—ourselves.

Adults are supposed to be different than children.

Time, experience, and physical growth should produce maturity.

Maturity allows us to think rationally, put things in context, and understand what is and isn't important.

My six-year-old cries when he doesn't get a toy because he is immature. He doesn't understand there will be more toys, more opportunities, and even if he doesn't get a toy, life will go on.

One aspect of maturity is discernment. A mature person has the ability to distinguish one thing from another. What an immature person sees as being the same things, a mature person can distinguish as having differences.

Discernment: a Forgotten Sign of Adulthood

We have lost all ability to distinguish one from another. And so we assume:

- If something is right for you, it must be right for me.
- If something worked for me, it must work for you.
- If a decision has a good outcome, it must be right.
- If a decision has a bad outcome, it must be wrong.

The nuanced, complex world, which requires intense thinking has been reduced to a simplistic, black-and-white world, which only requires our gut (and rarely our minds) in order to make a good decision.

Our inability to discern has disastrous consequences:

It produces debt. Because we can't discern what is right and wrong for us as individuals, we assume if a friend can afford something, so can we. We never consider how our finances differ from theirs. We never see the negative consequences of owning more things. Instead, we see something a friend has and we want it. Foolishly, we purchase things we can't afford all because we cannot discern wise spending from foolish spending.

It produces addiction. We see a friend engage in activities or behaviors that seem enjoyable and we never consider our temptations or weaknesses. It seems unfair to abstain from alcohol when others enjoy it. It seems prudish to avoid the casinos when our friends are going there on Friday night. When we fail to understand that we are tempted in ways others are not, we let our guard down. If someone lives within wise financial principles, a trip to Vegas can be great fun. Yet if someone struggles with a gambling addiction, the same trip can destroy them. When we fail to discern our strengths and weaknesses, we open ourselves up to addiction.

It produces divorce. Many relationships end because a couple does not have the ability to discern what they need to do, or not do, in order to make the relationship flourish. By failing to understand what it takes to succeed, they fail. They might assume the failure is because of incompatibility or not marrying their soul mate, but often it's because of a lack of discernment.

Why Some Learn Discernment And Others Don't

Discernment is always learned through failure. There is no other way. It's possible to learn through the failings of others–we watch, seek to understand, and discern what could happen if we make similar mistakes. However, most of the time failure is learned through our own failings. We make a decision, fail, and have the opportunity to learn.

But just because we fail doesn't mean we will learn to discern. There is a key difference between those who fail and learn and those who fail and do not learn. If we blame our failures on someone or something other than ourselves, we will never learn true discernment. Blame removes the responsibility from ourselves and places it on someone else. While blaming is fun, it is never useful.

It's only by taking personal responsibility for our choices and decisions that we can learn to discern what is right and wrong;

what works and what doesn't; what is good for us and what is harmful. Those who own their decisions learn discernment; those who blame others do not.

What Does Discernment Look Like?

Discernment might reveal itself in different ways for different people, but there are a few common characteristics of those who have matured into adulthood and have the ability to discern:

Financial: Financial discernment means I make all financial decisions based on my income, savings, debt, and personal goals for the future. I do not buy and spend based on the spending habits of my friends or co-workers. I recognize some can afford things I cannot. I recognize some will choose to spend their money in ways I do not. As a Christian, I recognize my giving to others will limit the dollars I can spend on myself.

Relational: Relational discernment means I have the freedom to choose who my spouse, friends, and many times, who my bosses

"There is a key difference between those who fail and learn and those who fail and do not learn. If we blame our failures on someone or something other than ourselves, we will never learn true discernment. Blame removes the responsibility from ourselves and places it on someone else. While blaming is fun, it is never useful."

will be. I don't have to be in a relationship with people I do not want to be around. I'm free to accept or reject anyone. While I will serve and love all people, I will not partner with those in serious need. I will serve those in need, but I will marry and hire (or be hired) by those with a certain level of emotional health. (Of course through sickness or tragedy, the emotional health of a partner could change in an instant. That would not free me from my responsibilities of a partner. There are many things I will endure as a spouse or co-worker which I would willfully avoid if the circumstance revealed itself prior to a commitment being made.)

Spiritual. Spiritual discernment means I understand things are not always as they appear. What society calls good, God may call bad. What God commands, culture may mock. Spiritual discernment seeks to allow God to define right and wrong. We then attempt to be unmoved by what others say or believe.

Discernment is a sign of adulthood. It is the result of maturity. Discernment protects us from foolish choices and bad decision making. It allows us to understand the world and those around us. It provides peace and enjoyment with what we have and what we do not have. It gives us a deep appreciation for the good things in life while softening the hurt of those things that are bad.

Sadly, discernment has become a lost art. Many are failing to mature, which results in a good number of people who physically are adults but emotionally and socially are children. Don't fall for the trap. The world is not always simple. You are not always right. Issues are not always black and white. No one is totally perfect or completely evil.

Life is complex. Issues are nuanced. Everybody is both good and bad. These realities demand discernment from us. And discernment is only possible when we take ownership for our lives and seek to learn how to make better decisions.

My dog has an annoying habit: whenever I try to come inside, she gets right in front of me, sits down, and puts her snout on my leg.

It's clearly a cry for attention. With two small kids, we do not give our outside dog enough attention. She's starved for it and when she actually receives attention, she longs for more. She desires so much more, she doesn't want me to go inside.

Of course when she puts her snout on my leg, her slobbery nose gets all over my pants. It's frustrating. Before I go outside, I have to check my closet and my watch to see if I have the clothes and the time to play with my dog.

My dog's actions have one effect—they make me less likely to spend time with her.

Notice the irony: what my dog does in hopes of getting me to spend more time with her is causing me to spend less time with her. Her actions are having the reverse effect of her intention.

As it is with her, so it is with many of us. Many times our actions have the reverse effects of our intentions.

The man, so desperate for a relationship, falls in love after every first date, scaring away any sane, healthy, emotionally-aware woman.

The woman, in such need for one sale, nearly attacks every potential client, causing them to avoid every contact with her.

The waiter, trying to make a personal connection in order to get a big tip, won't leave the couple on a date alone long enough for them to have a real conversation, which frustrates the man as he signs his ticket.

The car dealer so afraid of not being a pushy salesman, becomes so hands-off that people do not think he truly wants their business.

More often than we realize, our actions can actually have the reverse effect of our intentions. Imagine a gardener who so desperately wants a seed to grow that she over waters the garden. In her eyes, she is giving every waking minute to her garden. What she doesn't realize is that she is actually preventing it from growing.

This is the scenario for many people in business, friendships, and especially, intimate relationships.

When one relationship fails we can fairly assume it was just the circumstances of life. However, whenever we see a repeated pattern in our lives, our attention must turn to ourselves and we must ask, "What are we doing to contribute to this pattern?"

If you want to be married, but you are never dating—what are you doing that is preventing you from connecting with others?

If you have been married several times and all the relationships have had similar failed outcomes—how do you continually make bad choices of whom to be in a relationship with?

If you go from church to church, or group to group, looking for friends but you can't seem to connect with anyone, what are you doing that is preventing you from making good connections?

Way too often, we are quick to blame others, curse circumstances, or define groups as being full of cliques, but we are not quick to consider our own actions, review our own tendencies, and see how we are contributing to a problem.

Rarely are we solely responsible for bad outcomes, but rarely are we void of any responsibility.

In nearly every circumstance we play a role in failure. And when a pattern repeats itself in our lives with different people being involved, we are the common denominator.

I've met many people who are great at marriage, but horrible at choosing a mate. Of course the result is always divorce. It's not until they recognize their weaknesses and get help in those areas that they can then experience the happiness they desire.

Are there patterns of failure in your life? Are there outcomes you've experienced in the past which you do not want to repeat?

If so, what is the common thread in every situation?

And what are you doing to contribute to the problem?

Sometimes, not all the time, but sometimes, you are the one truly preventing you.

Sometimes, not all the time, but sometimes, you are the one truly preventing you.

Every day we wear multiple hats. We are employees, spouses, parents, citizens, cheerleaders, taxi cab drivers, counselors, teachers, advocates, and hundreds of other things.

On the average day we can wear every hat necessary to make sure our marriage functions, our kids thrive, and every responsibility is met.

But sometimes we can't.

There are moments in which it is impossible to wear multiple hats. Sometimes we can only wear just one.

As parents age, adult children often wear the hat of child and caregiver. It's an honor to return the care that our parents have given us. Yet a time comes when the ailing parent needs more than a part-time caregiver. In that moment, the faithful son or daughter must choose which hat to wear.

As kids play, Dads often wear the hat of father and coach. It's great fun to be on the field while our kids compete. Yet a time comes when the role of a dad requires love and support while the role of a coach requires commands and demands. In that moment, the dad must choose which hat to wear.

There are two primary reasons why sometimes we can only wear one hat:

1. **Conflict of interests.** At times the two responsibilities are at odds. This is often the case when coaching our children. What's good for the team and what's good for the child are not always the same thing. The legal and medical professions have clear guidelines for avoiding conflicts of interest. They know that relationships can cloud our judgment, and extreme caution

should be used when mixing professional relationships with private ones.

2. **Amount of available energy.** We can only do so much. Our resources are not unlimited. Whenever we are wearing multiple hats, we must frequently determine if we're doing each one justice. In the midst of the chaos of life, it is easy to give a second-rate effort to our most important tasks because we are expending our energy in other places.

Some Hats We Should Refuse...

Sometimes we don't have to choose which hat to wear, because one of the hats should never be worn.

We should never wear the hats of spouse and spouse's parent. It happens far too often. Do not try to be your spouse's parent. You don't want to be that and they don't need you to be that. Be the spouse. Do the things that spouses should do. Do not be the parent.

We should never wear the hat of enabler. We can, and should, be loving and kind, but it is never our responsibility to take away the natural consequences of the bad decisions of others.

We should never wear the hat of Savior. There is a God and we are not Him. We can assist others, but we cannot play the role of God.

The Most Important Rule of Hats...

When you have to choose, ALWAYS choose the most important hat. It sounds simple, but it's often not accomplished.

The easiest way to determine which hat to choose is to ask the question: are there any hats that only I can wear?

After my grandmother died and my grandfather was sick, my mom was his primary caregiver. As his health declined, it became a full-time job. She struggled with whether or not to put him in the nursing home, despite his clear wishes of never going to a nursing home. Being one generation removed from the situation, it was an obvious choice to me. I told my mom, "There are a thousand people who can be his caregiver, but only you can be his daughter."

He needed both people and neither would be a part-time job. We could find someone to be his caregiver, but only she could be his daughter.

When life forces us to choose roles, always choose the role which is the most important.

Many people could coach your kid, but only you can be their dad.

Many people can counsel your child, but only you can be their mom.

Many people can teach your wife or husband, but only you can be their spouse.

Most often, we can wear multiple hats on a daily basis and the world keeps moving, but there are times in life when we have to choose. We can't do both. When you can only wear one hat, make sure you pick the most important one.

"When you can only wear one hat, make sure you pick the most important one."

I love hearing a baby crying in a restaurant.

I love it because one thought comes to mind— it's not my responsibility.

At home, a cry demands my attention. I have to make decisions. I have to decipher the need and find an appropriate response. When my kid cries, I have to deal with it. When your kid cries, you have to deal with it.

A kid crying in a restaurant reminds me that not every crisis is my responsibility. Not every situation requires my judgment. In many situations, I get to stay out of the details and simply love the people and hope for their best.

As a problem solver, if I'm not careful I can be quick to run to a crisis. That's a good quality. The world is in desperate need of problem solvers. Yet the danger in being someone who solves problems is that I can be tempted to become involved in every crisis, even situations which are none of my business.

Instead of involving ourselves in every scenario, we should always make sure that we have a right and a responsibility to be involved. Sometimes we have neither.

When something isn't our job we should rejoice. We should be grateful the responsibility doesn't fall on us. We should enjoy our ability to stay neutral. We should be reminded that in many situations we have the ability to do nothing. We are often in the spotlight with the high expectation of being the person who can solve a crisis. Being alleviated of that responsibility on certain occasions should bring us great joy.

However, at the point in which we should rejoice, many of us don't. Even though it isn't our job, we make it our job. We worry. We choose sides. We feel the pressure to determine what happened and who is at fault.

We overstep our bounds and try to play a role that is not ours to play.

One of the most coveted positions in life should be neutrality. It is a great place to be.

"As a problem solver, if I'm not careful I can be quick to run to a crisis. That's a good quality. The world is in desperate need of problem solvers. Yet the danger in being someone who solves problems is that I can be tempted to become involved in every crisis, even situations which are none of my business."

We get to be neutral in many situations:

- When two business partners split ways, we don't have to pick sides. We simply have to be friends with each person to the best of our ability.
- When a divorce happens, a judge can determine how things should be divided; we don't have to determine fault.
- When good people disagree, we don't have to dig for details to determine who was wrong.

Sometimes we have to play the role of judge and jury, but many times we don't. Having to choose a side is difficult. Knowing the difficulty should make us thankful for the times we don't have to. It should keep us out of many situations because we know the stress they bring.

Life is often not as difficult as we make it.

Consider how many situations in which you're currently involved that don't actually require your involvement.

- Office drama
- A squabble between friends
- A community division in another town
- PTA politicking
- The latest gossip at the barber shop

Far more often than we realize, our only job is to love. Don't judge. Don't dig for details. Don't pick sides. Don't try to figure it all out. Simply love.

The next time you hear a baby crying in a restaurant, don't get irritated. Take a deep breath and say "thank you." Be grateful that at least one problem is not your responsibility. Then consider how many other situations in your life don't require anything but your love.

Sometimes I get tired of being nice.

I fantasize about what it would be like to:

- give people a piece of my mind
- say whatever I want to say
- return a rude action with a rude action
- hang up on someone
- yell at someone
- never speak to someone again

But it's all a fantasy. In the end, I do my best to be loving, kind, thoughtful, and measured in every action I take. While I fail often, I try to be nice.

Yet I grow tired of it.

Niceness is part of the pastorate, or at least it should be. Not every pastor is nice, but then again, not everyone who is a pastor should be a pastor.

A pastor should be nice, but that's not because of the job; it's because all people should be nice.

However, pastors and people alike grow weary of this niceness on occasion. We think and often say, "I'm tired of being nice."

Whenever I say that, I have properly identified a problem, but I have wrongly assumed the solution.

The truth is, whenever I feel tired of being nice, I'm actually tired of being a hypocrite. I've grown weary of my outward actions not matching my inward desires.

The tension between the two is a problem, and I'm right in believing the tension shouldn't exist.

But I'm wrong in thinking the solution to the problem is in being less nice. The last thing I need to be is less nice.

What I need to be is more loving, kind, generous, merciful, understanding, and empathetic. And I need my heart to desire more of these things.

The weariness I feel is not from being nice; it's from being a hypocrite.

Being a hypocrite is exhausting. We have to fake an action while feeling something completely different. The dichotomy creates tension and the tension exhausts all energy.

While hypocrisy is troubling, what's more troubling is when I blame other people for my failings. When I feel tired of being nice, what I'm actually believing is that other people are exhausting me. I think they are my problem and they are lucky at how kind I'm treating them.

So I'm a hypocrite who believes everyone else is wrong while I'm right and the only reason we continue to have a peaceful relationship is because of my kindness.

This thinking might make me feel better, but it's not true.

Whenever I grow weary of a good action, it's a reminder that something is wrong with my heart. Some aspect of who I am is not in line with who I want to be. The problem is not my action, but my heart.

Knowing this truth changes my perspective when weariness comes. I still feel the tension, but I tell myself the truth. I'm not tired of being nice. I'm tired because my heart is not as kind as I want it to be.

I must continue to restrain my wrong desires, act in a kind and loving way, and find ways to transform my heart.

Are you tired of being nice? Good. Your weariness can be a teacher which reveals a heart that's in need of change.

The next time you find yourself fantasizing about what you can do in response to another person, stop, pray, consider what that reveals about your heart, and change your response.

"Whenever I grow weary of a good action, it is a reminder that something is wrong with my heart. Some aspect of who I am is not in line with who I want to be. The problem is not my action, but my heart."

You won't change until you are sick of it.

Disgusted by it. Tired of it. Willing to do whatever it takes to change it. Unwilling to keep doing the same thing.

Until you get so sick of the...

addiction

bad marriage

failure

mediocrity

apathy

...nothing will change.

You might make promises. You might try to do better. But meaningful change will not occur.

It takes getting to this point for one reason—until you are absolutely sick of what's happening you will be more concerned with your reputation than getting better. As long as you're more focused on perception than health, you will not heal.

As a pastor of a church that offers many programs to assist people changing their lives, I regularly receive phone calls asking for copies of the materials those classes use. When they ask for those materials, I tell them we can mail the materials to them, but it won't help. The people are often surprised I say that, but I explain to them:

1. Meaningful change rarely happens in isolation. We need a healthy community in order to truly change. When someone seeks transformation in isolation, experience tells us it will not happen. That's why every weight loss program, exercise program, and recovery program includes a counselor, accountability person, and/or other people who are going through the same process. We need others in order to change. Trying to change in isolation does not work.

2. Meaningful change never happens until we're willing to admit we have a problem. Many times the reason someone wants to work on an issue in private is because they're unwilling to admit their problems to others. Until they're willing to call a pastor, make an appointment with a counselor, or admit to friends they need help, they will not get well.

Everyone has issues that they wish were different. Some go year after year with the same problem. They try to make changes. They make resolutions and promises only to fail over and over again.

Yet some people change. They get clean and sober, start working out, or make meaningful steps in their careers or families.

The difference between the two groups can often be narrowed down to one issue: those who change do so because they got sick and tired of their issue and were willing to do whatever it took to change. The others wanted to change, but were not willing to humble themselves, get help, do the work, and do what it takes to heal.

What are you tired of?
Are you weary enough to do what it takes to get better?
Who are you going to call to get help?
Are you dialing right now?

Notes

3

Decision Making

We are bad at decision making. Dr. Seuss said, "Simple it's not, I'm afraid you will find, for a mind maker-upper to make up his mind."

Seuss was right.

What we do matters. Our lives matter.

Because our lives matter, our decisions matter.

We are some of the few people to have ever lived whose lives are primarily determined by our own decisions.

- We choose whom we marry.
- We choose what we do.
- We choose where we live.

Never has anyone had as much control over their lives as we have, yet it's possible that no people have ever been as unhappy as most of us are.

Even though we choose whom we marry, divorce rates are high.

Even though we choose where we work, job satisfaction rates are low.

Even though we choose most aspects of our lives, many people are not happy.

The Good News: Never has humanity's decisions mattered so much.

The Bad News: We are bad at decision making.

Doubt this?

Go to Walmart on a Friday night and realize—every person in the store made a conscious decision of what to wear in public.

Still doubt this?

Consider every person you ever voted for. At the time, you thought it was a good decision.

Still don't believe?

Must I bring up your ex-husband or the girl you used to date or your excitement over the hiring of that coach?

Humanity is bad at decision making.

When given more control of our lives, humanity doesn't necessarily become happier, satisfied or content.

Obviously, the answer isn't to give control of our lives over to others.

The answer is to become better at decision making.

So:

- How many books have you read about decision making?
- How many classes or seminars have you attended?
- How much research have you done to make better decisions?

For most of us, the answer is none.

When it comes to decision making, I want to be a contrarian.

I want to make decisions in a way that is contrary to how most people think.

Why be contrarian? Because humanity is bad at decision making.

What makes sense to us is often wrong.

Here are four examples:

1. **We should not follow our hearts.** Few things are more deceitful than our own hearts. Society says to listen to them; I say lead them. Our hearts need to be guarded and guided, not followed.

2. **Love your friends, but don't listen to them.** Generally speaking, your friends are no smarter than you. So why should we listen to them? Friends are supposed to support us, to walk with us through our lives. They are not called to be our closest advisers. For that, we need someone smarter than us and our friends. Watch the game with your friends, but follow the advice of your advisers.

3. **We should ignore outcomes and focus on processes.** Outcomes matter, but processes are far more important. Outcomes reveal one decision, processes are the way every

decision is made. I'm far more concerned with making a decision the right way than making the right decision.

4. **If you don't like your decision, change your mind.** We fool ourselves into thinking we only get one shot at making a right decision. When choosing to donate a kidney or sky dive that might be accurate, but with most decisions we can change our minds. If you don't like the outcome, change it. We make the best decision we can, see how it goes, and then undo it if we don't like the outcome.

Decision making is far too important for us to assume we are good at it. We aren't. It is a skill we need to learn, but learning starts with humility.

Decision making is far too important for us to assume we are good at it. We aren't. It's a skill we need to learn, but learning starts with · humility.

There are some things you should
freak out about:

Your spouse is cheating.

Your child is missing.

Your lab reports show cancer.

In these and many other moments, it is perfectly understandable
for you to lose your mind.

On occasion, life throws situations our way that overwhelm every
capacity we have to understand and make a decision. In those
moments we have to trust others and receive their assistance in
navigating life's challenges.

But those times are rare.

For every other situation the very first thing which needs to happen
is you need to STOP FREAKING OUT.

Truth be told, you need to stop freaking out in the other situations
as well. As difficult as they are, freaking out will not help, but at
least it is understandable when a major event drives you crazy.
It doesn't make as much sense when people flip out over the
common issues.

News flash: Life will be full of difficulties.

Expect them. Don't be shocked by them. If ever there is a moment
when something isn't happening, don't be deceived into thinking
nothing is going on. Be wise enough to understand you simply
don't know about it yet.

Life never goes exactly as we plan. Every day will have challenges
which will require you to alter your plans and figure out a new
path.

Deal with it. And whatever you do, STOP FREAKING
OUT.

Notice: You will not make a wise decision if you're panicked. It's impossible. It won't happen.

Far too often, you and I freak out over a situation. The situation itself isn't that dramatic, and it's something we could reasonably navigate if we would simply keep our wits about us. However, the situation turns disastrous when we try to handle it in a panicked state.

Has your child made a bad choice?

Did your spouse forget to do something?

Did a business mess up your order?

Did an employee make a mistake?

Did your boss use the wrong tone?

All of these are situations we have to handle, but they are not things that should throw us for a big surprise.

Very few things should shock us.

Consider:

How prone we are to making mistakes.

How difficult it is to communicate.

How easy it is to make wrong assumptions.

Life will be complicated. Things will not go as we wish. We must expect it and not be freaked out.

Those who have the ability to make decisions from a calm mindset will far outperform those who make decisions from a chaotic mindset.

As a pastor, I see people in a variety of situations. What strikes me is how little it takes for some people to have their lives flipped upside down. While I'm watching young people battle disease or parents deal with the addiction of a child, others are distraught because life's small situations are not going their way—a grade isn't what it should be or a spouse isn't as perfect as we want or a boss makes decisions we don't like.

While I recognize these things can challenge us, they shouldn't destroy us. They shouldn't even greatly surprise us.

You can either accept it and try to navigate it in the best way possible, or you can freak out. The former will lead to a peaceful and purposeful decision making process; the latter will lead to utter chaos.

Decision making is a process. While it is not always the same for every problem, there are many common steps.

Step one, with any problem, is simple— stop freaking out so you can start figuring out what needs to be done.

Some decisions matter more than others.

Few, if any, remember what they had for lunch five years ago today. But every person can distinctly remember their wedding day, no matter how many wedding days they have had. I regularly tell couples at a wedding, "For better or worse, this will be a day you never forget." Getting married is always an important decision. Where you shop, what you eat, and how you spend some free time is generally not that vital.

Since some decisions matter more than others, the effort we put into making decisions should not be the same for every issue. Some choices deserve more time and effort than others.

One of the first things we have to determine is the context of the choice before us.

Determining the context and consequences of a decision reveal how much time and energy should be spent in the decision-making process. If the consequences are not extreme, little time needs to be spent on a decision. However, if the wrong choice could be disastrous, we must take adequate time to make the best decision possible.

Understanding the context of the decision determines nearly everything.

The context of a decision can be determined by asking five questions:

1. **Is this my decision to make?** Every Fortune 500 board, non-profit board, leader, and person should begin every discussion with this question—Is this our decision to make? Many times the answer is no. Even as a leader or parent, while the buck might stop with us, we must empower employees or children to make decisions. The fewer decisions we make, the better. And many decisions we fret over aren't even ours to make. Before spending any time on a decision, ask if this is yours to make.

2. **How important is the issue?** Nick Saban, head football coach for the University of Alabama, eats the same thing for breakfast and lunch every day—oatmeal cream pies for breakfast and a salad for lunch. Do you know why? He doesn't want to waste time debating what to eat. He knows he has to eat; he knows it doesn't greatly matter what he eats (although his doctor might disagree with his breakfast); so why waste time thinking about what doesn't matter when he can use that time thinking about things that do. If the issue isn't of great importance, don't spend a tremendous amount of time. Decide and move on.

3. **How difficult is making a wise choice?** Many decisions are difficult for everyone, but some are easy for certain people and harder for others. We must understand how difficult it will be for us to make a wise choice. Do I have a history of making bad choices in this area? If so, I need to get help. Is this an area in which many friends and colleagues have struggled? If so, I need to be careful. If a wise choice can be made easily, I can quickly make a decision. If others have failed in this area, I might need to take more time.

4. **Could my personal bias sabotage my decision-making process?** Sometimes we are too close to a situation to think rationally about it. Surgeons aren't allowed to operate on their loved ones because of a lack of objectivity. We must be very careful when making decisions because we are rarely objective. The more invested or involved we are with a situation, the more hesitant we should be in boldly making a decision alone.

5. **What could be the lasting consequences?** The longer lasting the potential consequences, the more time and effort that should be given to the decision-making process. Hiring an employee should take more time than choosing a copier because the potential consequences are greater. If today's decision will matter ten years from now, it should get more focus than a decision that won't matter ten months from now.

Every decision is not equal. Some matter more than others. Identifying the most important decisions and spending the appropriate amount of time on those decisions can be the difference between success and failure.

Every decision is not equal. Some matter more than others. Identifying the most important decisions and spending the appropriate amount of time on those decisions can be the difference between success and failure.

Every week I interact with people on the worst day of their lives. At the funeral home, in the hospital, in the courtroom, at jail, or just in my office, I see people's lives in shambles.

Many times the turmoil is outside their control. A bad diagnosis, death, a poor decision by someone else—those are not things anyone can control. In those times I try to encourage them not to lose heart.

Yet many times someone's life is falling apart because of their own decision-making. Years of failing to invest in the marriage is now revealing itself. A long-held secret has been revealed. An addiction is ripping a family apart.

In those moments people come to my office wondering what they should do.

My advice is always the same:

Make one healthy decision, repeat, and don't stop repeating.

A bad decision is rarely one bad decision. It's almost always a series of bad decisions. Maybe we are not conscious of the decisions we are making, but someone doesn't suddenly have an affair, hit the rock-bottom of an addiction, or lose all compassion. It happens slowly, as one decision leads to another. Eventually, bad consequences are experienced.

One of the first steps in helping people understand how their life got into a mess (assuming it was under their control) is showing them the series of decisions they made to get there. We take their attention off the final choice and highlight the hundreds of choices which led to that moment.

Once they see how the small choices led to big choices, they are prepared to start the process of healing. But the process is rarely one they like.

Whenever you believe your life went bad because of one decision, you can fall for the deception that your life can be made good by one decision. It never happens this way.

In the same way that life rarely goes wrong with one decision, it never goes right with one decision. It takes hundreds of right decisions to repair what hundreds of bad decisions have done.

One counseling session will not fix a marriage that has been bad for three years.

One workout will not undo years of inactivity.

One healthy day of eating will not undo months of poor eating.

You have to walk as long in the right direction as you did in the wrong direction, in order to make progress.

Sadly, many people are not willing to do so.

They will try faith for a day, but then give up.

They will choose wisely for a moment, but then return to foolishness.

They will flash diet for the week, but then return to the buffet.

They think one good decision can undo a series of bad decisions. It can't.

Yet it does all begin with a good decision. Until a person makes a single good decision, they do not have the ability to heal, grow, or succeed. One decision can't make it happen, but it does all start with a single decision.

Whenever I talk with someone whose life is in shambles, my main goal is to help them make a single good decision. What is the next step they need in order to walk toward wisdom and health? Once they make that decision, they simply need to repeat the process.

Make a good decision. Repeat. Don't stop repeating.

Who do you want to be in one of those moments?

You know "those moments."

The moments:

- when the stakes are high and the choices are serious.
- which define not just individuals, but whole families, companies, and communities.
- which cause most people to make bad choices, lose reputations, and to fold under pressure.

We all want to be the type of people who are the same no matter the situation. We want to be the ones others can lean on in difficult times. We want to lead when everyone else is afraid. We want to maintain character when everyone else is losing theirs.

But how?

It's tempting to believe that the difference between those who lead through tough times and those who wilt under pressure is internal strength. And no doubt strength matters.

Yet the strength of good leaders and bad leaders isn't that different.

The difference is that good leaders know a secret that bad leaders do not.

The secret of being who you want to be when the moments matter the most is deciding who you will be before those moments occur.

Some decisions must be made before the questions are asked.

You can't wait for the moment.

If you wait, you might make a good choice—once or twice, maybe three times. But if you wait, you're risking disaster. Eventually you will choose poorly.

You must not wait.

You must decide now who you will be then.

So often the difference between those who make wise choices and those who do not is not inner strength, desire, or willpower. It's timing. Often, someone makes the wrong decision because they made it too late. They waited until the pressure was on, and because of that, chose poorly.

Others choose to:

- Be a faithful spouse before they ever feel the temptation to stray.
- Be an honest salesperson before they have the opportunity to cheat a prospect.
- Record their true score before they ever hit the tee shot.
- Love whomever crosses their path.
- Serve no matter what is demanded.

By making the choices before facing the temptation, they remove the stress, pressure, and temptation of the moment. The choice is made solely on whom they want to be.

Making the choice beforehand, they greatly increase the likelihood of making a wise choice. It doesn't guarantee it. We can all ignore what we have said we would do and make dramatically different choices. But it does make it much easier to choose wisely.

For a company or organization, many of these choices are expressed through core values. They define what a company will or will not do depending on a situation.

In the same way that a company should define these values, individuals and couples should do the same.

- Who do we want to be?
- What do we want to value?
- How will we respond to the truth?
- How will we treat people?
- What will we refuse to be associated with?

In a moment of pressure, any of us could make a foolish choice. Yet when we take the time to answer these questions before a situation occurs, we are more likely to choose wisely.

"So often the difference between those who make wise choices and those who do not is not inner strength, desire, or willpower. It is timing. Often, someone makes the wrong decision because they made it too late. They waited until the pressure was on, and because of that, chose poorly."

Never make a decision until you have to.

There are some decisions which need to be made now. To wait is to risk. If you do not make the decision now, you will likely make a poor decision later. It's true with exercise, money, food, character, and a host of other issues.

You should decide right now what you will eat 12 hours from now. If you decide now, you will likely make the decision in light of the long-term perspective. You will choose healthier options and make wiser choices. If you wait until it's time to eat, you run the risk of poor choices. A greasy hamburger has much more sway over a person in the moment than 12 hours earlier.

You should not choose in the moment whether to get out of bed and exercise. The decision will be much more difficult. You will be tempted to continue to sleep. If you choose before going to bed what time you will get up and stick with that decision, you will make better choices.

You should choose right now the type of person you want to be. Don't wait until you have the choice to cheat to determine if you are the type of person who will cheat. Choose now, because you will choose better than if you wait until later.

Some decisions need to be made sooner.

Other decisions need to be made later. To act now is to risk. If you make the decision now, you will likely make a poor decision. More information will come with time. You will grow and mature. A delay might even remove the need to make a decision.

You should wait to make up your mind about people. Rarely is there a need to make a definitive early opinion. Get to know them. Understand their story. See who time proves them to be. Whether it be a new boss, your daughter's new boyfriend, or just someone you met, give it some time before boldly making up your mind.

"Some decisions need to be made sooner.

Other decisions need to be made later. To act now is to risk. If you make the decision now, you will likely make a poor decision."

You should wait to make up your mind about results. There is no need to judge the value of counseling, two sessions into counseling. There is no need to reevaluate an exercise plan a few weeks into the new lifestyle. I will often meet with people, determine a course of action, and a week later hear the person has completely given up on what we decided was best. "It wasn't working," they will say. "It's only been a week," I will respond. Wise choices often don't provide the immediate good feeling or outcome we desire. They are wise because of the long-term, not the short-term. This is what makes wise decision-making so difficult. Give it some time.

You should wait to make up your mind about a job. Don't feel pressure after the first interview to determine if you want the job or not. To do so puts you in a position of need and possibly desperation. At minimum it will negatively impact your negotiating ability. At a maximum it will cloud your judgment from discerning if the job is even a good fit.

Do not make a decision today that can be fairly made tomorrow. If there are consequences to waiting, then do not wait. Do not delay decision-making out of fear or laziness. Yet if there is no benefit to deciding something today, but there is benefit to delaying the decision, wait.

Steven Sample, in his book *The Contrarian's Guide to Leadership*, discusses what he calls "thinking gray." He says that as a leader it is important for him to refrain from forming an early opinion about something so that he can fairly evaluate all the facts. Humanity is prone to believe the first side of the story they hear. This often gets us in trouble.

By thinking gray, we keep an open mind about issues until it is time to make up our minds. When we decide too early, we close our minds to new information and we are biased toward any information we see. This results in poor decision-making.

Sadly, humanity often delays decisions they should make now and rushes decisions they could save for tomorrow. Unless we recognize this human tendency, we will fall for its trap. The result will be disastrous for us and others.

Don't decide until you have to.

I have a saying when it comes to golf—
"Whatever club you hit, hit it."

Club selection is important in golf. If you choose the wrong club, you have little opportunity to succeed. It makes the role of a caddy a vital one. A caddy is called to assist a player in making a wise decision. They can talk the player out of the wrong club and convince them of the right club.

However, many shots can be played several ways. There isn't necessarily one right way. Several clubs may be wrong, but a few clubs could be right. While a player has to pick one of the right clubs, they also have to execute the shot. Oftentimes a player will fail to commit to the shot they hit and assume they picked the wrong club. The club wasn't wrong; the execution was faulty.

Whatever club you hit, hit it. Execute the shot you have chosen to play.

It is true in golf and it's true in leadership.

Decision-making is vital. It's an often overlooked art in the world of leadership. In a day where we have more decision-making power than ever, we spend less time learning and teaching the proper way to make wise choices.

Yet making the right decision isn't everything.

An important part of good leadership is also about making the decision right.

As a leader, I can look back on projects and new ventures we started which did not go as we had hoped. At times, we made bad decisions. We got so caught up in what we thought could happen that we overlooked the reality of what we were dealing with. The bad choices led to bad outcomes. Yet there are other times when I still believe we made the right decision. Others have made the same decisions we made and experienced far better outcomes than we did. We failed not at making a right decision, but at making the decision right. We put so much time and energy into the decision-making process, but then dropped the ball on the execution of the decision we made.

It doesn't matter what decision you make if you do not make the decision right.

If you fail to execute the plan, do the work, and adapt as conditions change, no amount of right decision-making will lead to the outcome you desire.

I've seen many individuals wisely choose a good mate. They did everything they could to make a right decision, but their marriage failed. It didn't fail because they married the wrong person; it failed because they didn't do the work necessary to make the marriage thrive. They made the right decision but didn't make the decision right.

There are two ways to have a bad outcome:

1. **Fail to make a right decision.** Assume whatever you decide will work. Be deceived into thinking the decision is easy. Fail to do your homework, study the issues, find multiple options, and choose the right one.

2. **Fail to make the decision right.** Assume after you've made a right decision, the rest is easy. Get lazy. Fail to adapt. Stop paying attention to changing landscapes.

In golf you have to pick the club that can give you the best outcome, but you also have to execute the shot.

What's true in golf is true in life.

It always makes me nervous when I go through a gate with road spikes.

Even though an untold number of cars have safely passed through them, I always wonder if they have been installed correctly.

I figure I'll be the first person to legally pass through the gate only to have my tires explode because an installer turned the drawings upside down.

Gates have spikes to ensure that traffic only flows one way. You can't go in the exit and once you are out, you are out. There is no turning back.

Far too often, we look at decisions like gates with spikes.

We feel the pressure of making the right decision and approach it as though once we make the decision there is no turning back.

This is true with some decisions:

- getting married
- donating a kidney
- demolishing a building

With some decisions there is no turning back, but that isn't true with most decisions.

Most of the choices we have to make, can be unmade.

We can change our minds.

We can try something, see how it works, and try something else.

It's true of careers.

For a majority of people, if you don't like your current job, you can go back to school, get new training, and find something else. Sure, it will take a lot of work, effort, and money, but the opportunity is there.

The vast majority of decisions that cause us to fret, are decisions which can be undone if we get them wrong.

This fact should free us.

It shouldn't cut down our work or ease the decision making process, but it should give us greater confidence in making a decision.

With most choices—even big ones—we are not jumping out of an airplane. If we walk through the door and wish we hadn't, we can turn around and walk right back through it.

"Most doors swing both ways," a mentor tells me. It's true and it's liberating.

Take your time.

Choose wisely.

Understand that mistakes can be costly.

But don't worry so much about the outcome that you're paralyzed from ever making a decision.

Even if you get it wrong, you can make it right.

Even if you can't make it right, you can un-make most decisions and try again.

The good news with trying again is that you are a little bit wiser the second time than the first.

The vast majority of decisions that cause us to fret, are decisions which can be undone if we get them wrong.

This fact should free us.

People mean well.

- The co-worker who has a cousin that went through a similar situation as you.

- The friend who has an uncle who had a great result.

- The mother-in-law who has a bit more experience in raising kids than you.

They mean well.

They desire what is best for you, your family, your children, and everyone involved.

They mean well which is why they invade your privacy, give advice you have not asked for, and butt in even though they have not been invited.

What do you say in moments like these?

How can you be kind, courteous, and yet clear that this is your decision and not theirs?

I have a line I've found works very well with these persistent people.

Say, "We are happy with our decision, thank you."

It works in a variety of situations:

- When grandma critiques how you parent
- When a friend thinks you are too strict
- When your cousin thinks you should get a second medical opinion
- When your father-in-law doesn't like how you spend money
- When someone doesn't like how you vote

Some would say this is too simple. Many people are far too persistent for one little sentence to convey the proper message. Yet I have found it to be very effective.

I say it the first time, "We are happy with our decision, thank you," and I mean it. I'm grateful the person cares enough to say what they need to say. I'm happy to be able to share with them our contentment while thanking them for their courage to attempt to help.

If they persist, I say, "We are happy with our decision, thank you."

The second time I say it, I'm making it clear that our mind is made up. It is our decision, we have made it, and we are not changing our mind unless we decide to do so.

When they persist, I say, "We are happy with our decision, thank you." The third time I say it, I'm clearly communicating that we will not be discussing this issue. I'm all for discussion, but I'm for discussion with the people whose business it is to discuss the issue. I'm against discussion with people who have no right or responsibility for the decision.

Whenever I say there is one statement which will keep others from invading their privacy, most people don't believe me. I understand their doubt.

However, time has proven this one statement to be effective. I've yet to hear of a situation where the other party didn't eventually get the message, even if it had to be repeated a few times.

We all need help. We all need insight from others. Yet many things are our responsibility. We have to make the best decision possible and other people have to allow us to. "We are happy with our decision, thank you," assists us in dealing with well-meaning people.

I have a line I've found works very well with these persistent people. Say, "We are happy with our decision, thank you."

Notes

4

Work

With fire. That's the best way to start your Monday.

Get to work. Don't enter the week apathetically. Don't slow play your way into your day.

Charge in like someone who has something to accomplish.

Most people make two major mistakes in starting their workday and their workweek:

1. They don't plan their work.
2. They try to ease into their day.

Both sabotage productivity.

Some don't have this privilege. Some jobs don't allow the worker to make choices. An ER doctor faces whatever patients might be in the room. A teacher must start when the bell rings. An airplane pilot will hit the throttle when the schedule demands it.

But many of us do have flexibility in our jobs. We get to determine what task should be our next one.

When flexibility is ours, intention must be our choice.

Nothing will increase our productivity and purpose as much as planning our day and charging into the most important tasks.

Do what matters.

The last way we should start our day is with a few small tasks that simply don't matter.

Checking email or returning unimportant phone calls is a setup for failure.

Many make the mistake of spending the opening minutes of their Monday catching up with co-workers—reviewing Friday night outings or Saturday's game. This might be good for friendship, but it's horrible for production. Wasting the opening minutes of a workday is procrastination. Beginning the day or week this way makes you more likely to continue the pattern throughout the week. When you begin behind, you will probably end behind.

There is a better way.

Determine the most important thing.

By defining what the most important task is for your week and for your day, you set yourself up for success. Determine it and do it. Don't push it off until Tuesday. Don't wait until the afternoon. Determine what the task is and start attacking it. Ignore your email. Refuse phone calls. Tell your co-workers you will talk to them later.

Get to work.

Nothing will engage you more or make you feel more alive than finding a way to accomplish important things early in your day. By doing so, you're taking control of your day. Even if the rest of the day gets hijacked by an unexpected emergency, you will still leave the office with a sense of accomplishment.

Don't confuse activity with productivity.

Too often we begin our workdays with meaningless activity. I seriously doubt your email will reveal the most important task of your week. I doubt a little paperwork or filing a report is the most pressing issue. Yet when we confuse activity for productivity, we can deceive ourselves into thinking we are getting work done.

Everyone has small tasks that must be accomplished. Instead of doing them first, save them. Pile the small tasks together to be accomplished right before lunch or right before you go home. If you reach a breaking point on your big task, then change mental gears by knocking out several minor responsibilities.

But don't start your day with something that won't matter tomorrow.

Your brain needs more than that. Your heart needs to be engaged from the get-go.

Love your co-workers, but talk to them later.

Some of your co-workers may not like this approach. They might think you're rude. They may be threatened by your work ethic. They might be confused by your intention.

However, the most loving thing you can do is to refuse to review the weekend. There will be a time for that. I'm not saying to be cold or uncaring. You should listen and understand what's going on in the lives of those around you. But Monday morning is not when that should take place. Save it for lunch or a coffee break or at the end of the day when you're mentally drained. Make your personal connections, but don't try to make them at the start of the day.

> When the day is brand new and the whole week is before you, take on the most important task with your best energy.

Chances are, if you have the freedom to choose how to do your work, then someone is paying you to make those choices. Honor them by making wise ones. Don't fall for the sucker's choice of doing the easiest thing or the most time-sensitive item or the task another person is complaining about. Choose the most important thing and engage your body, mind, and soul.

Do that today, tomorrow, every day, and watch how differently you approach work.

If you have a job, you're getting paid to do two things: figure out what's important and do it.

For most people, reading a book on time management is a waste of time. It's a distraction from what they should actually be doing.

A majority of writers who buy books/software/products on publishing are creatively dodging actually writing a book.

Nearly every meeting held at work has little to no impact on moving a company or employees ahead.

Why?

Why do we dream more than we do? Why do we meet at length, planning how to get our work done, but actually accomplishing little work?

The answer is simple... people like to talk about work far more than actually doing work.

The difference between success and failure for the average person is the difference between talking about work and doing work.

Successful people get work done. Everyone else talks about doing work.

While some are blatantly lazy and will admit it, most of us are unknowingly lazy. We find ways to make ourselves and others believe we're doing important things when in actuality, we are avoiding what needs to be done.

Consider the process: We feel as though we're working hard but we aren't accomplishing anything.

It's the same scenario many people go through regarding decision-making. They have a decision to make, but instead of taking steps to gather information in order to make an intelligent decision, they worry. Worrying feels like they're dealing with the issue, but it doesn't get them any closer to making up their mind. They feel they're working but with no progress.

> The difference between success and failure for the average person is the difference between talking about work and doing work.

So it is with how most of us work. We fill our days with tasks that look like work, but they're not actual steps to accomplishing what really matters.

We end up exhausted, but have accomplished nothing. We're worn-out, but worthless.

The difference between those who do the work and those who talk about doing the work is in how they handle distractions.

No matter how well you plan your work and set aside time to accomplish what needs to be done, you face distractions. Those who do the work ignore the distractions; those who talk about doing work fall for the distractions. And often seek out distractions.

Imagine a husband and wife on a date. As they begin the meal, a beautiful woman approaches the table and with a sultry voice, looks at the man and says, "Can I borrow you for a moment?"

A wise man says, "No, I'm on a date with my wife."

But a foolish man looks at his wife and says, "She just needs me for a moment. I'll be right back."

So it is with our work. At every moment we're tempted to leave the work and interact with whatever opportunity presents itself in the moment.

A fool gives in.

A wise man holds fast to his commitments.

The difference between a productive day and an unproductive day is often found in our ability to ignore the distractions.

Assuming you have determined the most important tasks of your day, here's the best way to ignore all other temptations:

1. **Commit to the most important work.** It sounds simple, but making up your mind to do a project at a specific time can go a long way to pushing off all distractions. Write it down, say it out loud, or tell a co-worker what you're going to do. Then when distractions come, it will be easier to remember you've already committed to a certain task. Think about how easy it is to tell a co-worker, "I have a meeting," when they're asking you to do something. They're often quick to understand. If you commit to a certain task and put it on your calendar, you can tell every other distraction, "I'm sorry. I have a commitment."

2. **Schedule pockets for unforeseen work.** If you have a specific time set aside for tasks you haven't planned for, it will be easier to push those requests into that time rather than taking care of them in the moment. Get used to saying, "We can talk about this at ____," and, "I've scheduled ____ for that task." By having a specific place to put requests, we can avoid the temptation of dropping our important work for whatever is pressing in the moment."

3. **Be helpful, but do not do their work for them.** If we're skilled at getting work done, people will often turn to us with the hopes we'll do their work for them. While it is often tempting to do so, we must avoid the temptation. Offer people advice, but don't accept assignments from those who are not in authority over you. Doing the work of others will quickly lead to more people trying to hand their work off to you.

In the end, the task is simple. Do the work. Ignore everything else and do what needs to be done.

Originality is a mirage. The world is too big for anyone to truly be original. We are all copies of something or someone. Yet there is this thing we do. We take our God-given makeup and we use it to express ourselves, make money, spend time, raise kids, etc.

One of the most difficult aspects of growing up is trying to figure out who we are. When I was in college, a student asked our old professor a question about identity. The professor laughed and said, "Son, you won't even know your speaking voice until you are forty." It takes a long time to figure out who we are and what we want to do.

In order to learn, we try different things, emulate others, and search for who we want to be. Oftentimes, what we think we want and what we actually want aren't the same thing. There is no way for us to know this divide until we try. I always thought it would be fun to be a college professor until I started teaching adjunct classes. While I loved teaching, I couldn't stand grading papers, the extra demands on my time, and dealing with the paperwork. I thought I wanted to be a college professor, but when I was one, I didn't like it.

Part of growing up is trying new things, seeing what they're like, and determining who you want to be.

Once you figure out what you do, you should do it. Without explanation or apology, you should do what you do.

But know this–it won't be easy. At every turn you'll have two people pulling you to be something you're not.

The first threat is you. Doing what you do takes humility because you can't do everything. You have weaknesses. You can only do so many things. To choose one thing is not to choose something else.

Humility allows us to recognize our limitations, embrace them, and choose our actions.

Pride will tempt us to do more than we're able. It will cause us to overestimate our ability or importance. We won't be able to do what we do because we'll be trying to do everything.

Conversely, guilt can hinder us. We can assume our limitations and weaknesses are unique. We often underestimate the faults of our heroes. Whether they be a celebrity we don't know or a friend we deeply respect, we think their lives are more well put together than they actually are. We see their strengths, but fail to see their faults. Guilt tells us we should be better, do better, and accomplish more than what is humanly possible.

> The most important step in doing what you do, is allowing yourself to appreciate who you are and embrace what it is you do.

The second threat which may prevent you from doing what you do is others. Doing what you do takes courage because you will have to be able to endure criticism. Some are well-intended. Some are unaware that their criticism is damaging. Many are stifling the work of others in order to justify their own failures.

As a leader, I regularly have people telling me what I should be doing. Most of the time, what they're suggesting is a wonderful idea; it just doesn't fit who I am. On other occasions people assume you can add one more thing to your schedule or change some part of your personality without having any negative consequences. They fail to understand that every pro has its con.

Even on my website kevinathompson.com, people often comment that I should do something more or cover other topics. While many times their suggestions are good, in some instances they're asking me to do something I have strategically chosen not to do. While it would be fine for me to promote a political party or add Bible verses to every post, it's not what I want to do on this platform. To do so would be a change of strategy. It's not wrong for others to do those things, but it's not what I do. I need to do what I do.

And so do you.

At work. You have skills and abilities. You can't do everything, but you can do some things very well. Figure out how you best operate, find a job that best fits who you are, and do your very best. Don't regret that you aren't someone else. Don't be envious of others who have different skills. Do what you do.

In marriage. While healthy marriages may have common qualities, they have many different expressions. Work on your weaknesses, but don't be defined by them. If both partners are happy, the marriage is healthy, and you're headed in a good direction, accept that as a couple there are some things you don't do well and move on.

In parenting. Not every parent is the same. Don't feel pressure to have every strength of every good parent you know. There are some things my kids will not get from me. I wish it was different, but it's not. However, there are many good things they will get from me. As a parent, I need to do what I do to the best of my ability.

It sounds simple, but one of the most difficult aspects of life is deciding what you want to do and then doing it. To do so, not only will you have to do the work to figure out who you are, but you'll also have to have the humility to accept your limitations and the courage to ignore other people when they attempt to take you off course.

I hear it on a regular basis—"I could do the job."

Many times they believe it and often I believe them.

But then they continue, "They just won't give me a chance."

Believing you're being held back by others is a common experience. We all think we can do things if someone would just give us the opportunity. However, whenever that belief STOPS your action instead of motivating you to do MORE, you have a problem.

Everyone needs an opportunity. None of us would be where we are unless someone gave us a break. And oftentimes, it's a chance we didn't fully deserve.

But there is a difference between someone taking a small risk on us and someone ignoring all semblance of common sense to give us something we don't deserve. And there is a bigger difference between us hoping others will offer us help along the way and us doing nothing until someone gives us the chance we think we deserve.

Here is what people often forget: Getting the job is part of doing the job.

If you can't get the job, you can't do the job. We often believe people should give us an opportunity we don't deserve because we believe we can do the task at hand. Whether we can or can't isn't important. The fact is, if we can never get the job, it doesn't matter if we can do the job or not.

Part of doing the job is getting the job. Education often means very little as to whether someone can do a specific job, but it often means everything regarding whether someone will be able to get a specific job. What is true of education is often true of experience and a host of other characteristics which are often requested on a job application.

Some people see those requirements as hoops that must be jumped through in order to be able to show their ability, so they jump.

Others see those requirements as arbitrary obstacles that should be ignored as someone gives them their chance.

The requirements of a job can be debated, but the reality that every job has prerequisites is not a discussion. The question is, "Will you become bitter because of how you think life should be, or will you do what needs to be done in order to accomplish your dreams?"

Can't pass medical school? You can't be a doctor.

Can't attract readers? You can't make a living as an author.

Can't get an interview? You can't have the job you want.

Fair or not, it's reality. While it might be fun to curse the world for how it is and dream of how it should be, it's far more productive to figure out how things work and to do what's necessary to get what you want.

Many have great dreams about what they want to accomplish. However, they're not so passionate about doing what's necessary to make those dreams come true. Until they realize that getting the job is part of doing the job, it won't matter what skill set they may or may not have.

What do you want to do with your life? What are some prerequisites which must be accomplished before you will get the opportunity you're hoping for? What are you doing to get the job?

I was nine or ten when the Nintendo console finally made it to my hometown. What my own nine-year-old would find boring, mesmerized me and my friends for several years. But before the Nintendo, we had an Atari. We didn't play it much because it wasn't that exciting, but when we did play, we had two games—Pong and Pac-Man.

When I think about what the average employer is looking for, I think back to my childhood. We need less Pong and more Pac-Man.

Pong was a type of tennis game. You had control of a bar and your opponent had control of a bar. A ball bounced back and forth. The goal was to hit the ball back at your opponent, hoping they wouldn't be able to return it.

This describes the mentality of many modern workers. With a thousand responsibilities and little time, their number one goal is to bounce problems in another direction. Something arises and they direct it to a co-worker. The co-worker directs it back, so they take it to their boss. The boss bounces the problem back, so they pass it in a different direction. At all times they're bouncing problems in other directions.

Pac-Man had a different concept. A grid was filled with pellets and the object was for Pac-Man to eat all the pellets without being caught by one of the enemies. The goal was to eat all you could while avoiding the bad guys.

This should be the mindset of the modern worker. We get things done.

There is a time for Pong. Leaders need to have a Pong mentality when an employee presents a problem. We need to assist them, give them ideas, and empower them. We don't need to take their problems from them. We need to bounce the problems back to them while giving them tools to solve whatever issue they're having.

But most of the time we need to be like Pac-Man. We need to eat every problem that comes our way. Bouncing problems destroys efficiency; it wastes time; it causes us to spend more energy not solving problems than solving them. While it might shorten our to-do list, it does not lengthen the company's done list. Know this: An employer cares more about what you've done than what you have left to do. She cares more about what you've accomplished than what you passed on to others.

Sometimes you don't have a choice. A task is outside of your area of expertise, someone else is more involved in the situation, or policy dictates a certain procedure. But most of the time, the employee who first presented the problem can fix the problem.

Here are three steps to more Pac-Man and less Pong:

1. **Have the mindset of a problem-solver.** The biggest reason we bounce problems to others is because that's our primary mindset. We may not even realize it, but we're so afraid of being involved with the task that we pass it to another person. The fear could be a lack of time, energy, knowledge, or being held accountable for the outcome. But whatever the issue, we have to change our mindset. Decide to be a Pac-Man and you will see new issues as opportunities to chew on rather than situations to bounce to another person.

2. **Learn how to ask for help instead of passing the buck.** Whenever you need assistance, frame your question in a way

that ensures you stay in charge of the task. Simply stating a problem might cause a boss or co-worker to assume you want them to take over. But asking, "How would you suggest I handle this situation?" makes it clear you want to be the one to get the job done.

3. **Let your employer know you desire to grow in this area.** Most employers love employees who desire to grow. They will help them find the opportunities and resources to do so. If you see a "Pong" mentality within you, seek help. Let your direct supervisor know of your weakness and your desire to change. Chances are they already see the problem. Admitting it will show them you want to be different.

One caveat: Having a Pong mentality is advantageous if you're worried about job security. Pong employees rarely get in trouble. They're able to fly under the radar, always able to say who they passed a project to or who was supposed to handle an issue. Since they rarely do anything, they rarely get in trouble.

Pac-Man workers experience more risk. They make more mistakes and are more visible. But it's the Pac-Man employees who make a business run. They're the ones who get things done. If you want to be safe, consider Pong. If you want to make a difference, be Pac-Man.

As for me, I want less Pong and more Pac-Man.

It's not your boss' job.

If you have a boss, hopefully you have one who is sincerely concerned about you as a person. They care for you, your family, and your career. If you have one of those bosses, give thanks because not everyone does. Many people work for bosses who care nothing about them personally. Employees are seen as tools to be used until they no longer have value. If you have a good boss, be grateful and realize the rarity of your experience.

Yet even if your boss is good, your career is not their job. Hopefully, they consider it. On occasion they might even assist you with it, but make no mistake—it is not their job.

Your boss has too many responsibilities to be in charge of your career. While they have a moral obligation to assist you where possible, they are not responsible for it.

Too many employees believe their careers are in the control of the people they work for. This makes employees feel:

- trapped
- helpless
- unable to change their situation

That might have been the case forty years ago. There was a time when an employee worked for one company his entire career and one boss could make or break him, but that's no longer the case.

You are in charge of you.

While we all need assistance from others, one boss will not make or break our career.

The only person who will make or break you is you.

This is the problem for many employees—they want everything handed to them.

They believe if they wait their turn, put in their time, and do what they're told, they'll get the promotion, raise or responsibility they think they deserve. They think they're waiting on their boss.

Chances are, their boss is waiting on them.

Without a doubt, their career is waiting on them.

You are in charge of you and that is especially true in a culture where there's so much freedom for employees. While the choice is not solely up to an employee, they do play an equal role in agreeing to a working relationship. I'm not forced to work for a company I don't like, a boss I don't respect, or in a job I don't love. I'm free to quit anytime I choose. And I can pursue other opportunities at my own desire.

There are three major areas where my boss should assist me with my career, but in the end, I'm completely responsible for my own growth:

Knowledge. Never has there been a time when learning new information has been so readily available. If an employee isn't growing on their own, they're doing a disservice to themselves and their company. A boss might advise a good direction to learn new concepts, but an employee is responsible for doing the learning.

Experience. This is the area where people tend to be the most dependent on a boss. We think we can't gain experience until we're given an opportunity. We fail to recognize that experience can be gained in many ways. First, an employee should ask for more responsibility and experience. This will make their desire to grow evident. Yet even if their boss says 'no,' they can gain experience in other areas. Leadership skills can be developed by assisting non-profits or volunteering at a school. Understanding can grow as you learn from the experience of others—listening and evaluating what they're going through.

Skills. If you're waiting until you get a job to develop the skills necessary for the job, you will never have the skills or the title. The world has changed greatly and employees cannot delay learning new skills. This should be an ongoing process. Good companies assist the process, but good employees are always learning new skills no matter the expectations they have at work. Communities, colleges, universities, and non-profits are always offering free or inexpensive training. Some are technical, while others apply to any profession. Leadership, communication, public speaking, problem-solving, and decision-making skills are things that should be learned no matter what your job.

Many employees think their future is dependent on a boss or company. That might have been true a few decades ago, but that is not true today. You're in charge of your career. Learn, grow, and expand whether your boss helps you or not.

I was an employee today—all day. I woke up to a text message from someone in need and 15 hours later I came home just in time to put my son to bed.

These days are rare. I work for an organization that doesn't allow its staff to regularly work hours like I did today, but there are occasions when it's necessary.

I don't feel called to be an employee. It's what I do. I enjoy it, but it's not my calling.

It's where I currently express my calling, but it may not always be the place.

I feel called to use words to tell stories and express ideas. Speaking those words is the most fun, but writing them is enjoyable as well.

On most days I enjoy my job because it allows me to do what I love, but on some days it restricts my gifting.

Some days, like today, force me to shelve my heart's desire in order to do what others need. It's a privilege to help, but it's not something that brings my soul fully alive.

Today I was a employee, but at no point did I really use my gifts or live out my calling or do what I think God created me to do.

But the day isn't over. It's almost over, but a small amount remains.

I have a choice. I can either chalk this day up to one where I don't get to do what I truly love or I can get to work. Exhausted, mentally drained, and hoping that tomorrow is more productive, I can turn on my laptop, open a blank document, and begin to write.

The choice is mine.

I didn't have much of a choice today regarding my schedule, but I have 100 percent control over the next two hours. I can use them as I wish.

Every day I talk to people who have unfulfilled dreams. They feel as though they aren't living out their potential. They have callings they feel aren't expressed.

When we talk about their desires, they often describe their lives as being beyond their control. They want to do something, but they don't have time.

I nearly always ask, "What do you do at 10pm?"

For me it's the ultimate test.

> At the end of the day, when your job is over and the demands of your house are generally met, what do you do?

Few people understand the power of two hours a day. Whatever your dream, spending two hours a day on it will make it become a reality. Whatever your calling, spending two hours a day on it will bring you fulfillment. Whatever your talent, spending two hours a day on it will improve it.

When people say they don't have time, I don't believe them. We all have the same amount of time. Sure, there are busy seasons. No doubt there are days when we have few choices. But by and large, we will make time for what we want. Even if it means skipping dinner, losing sleep, and overlooking a dirty kitchen, we can at least work from 10 to 12 at night to do what we think we were created to do.

For too many people, they think their jobs are holding them back from their dreams. Stop using your job as your excuse. It pays the bills. It might allow you to express part of your gifting. It could teach you more skills than you would have otherwise. Your job is not the reason your dreams aren't coming true. Your unwillingness to work at the edges of the day—early in the morning or late at night—is the real reason you're not expressing your calling.

My life has been dramatically altered for the good by ordinary people who spent the edges of their day doing what they felt they were created to do. Some practiced music and every Friday night entertained me at a local restaurant. Some studied the Bible and taught my Sunday School class each week when I was a kid. Some coached little league teams and gave their time so I could learn a sport.

It wasn't their job, but their job paid the bills so they could spend their other hours doing what they enjoyed.

I enjoy what I do and I'm lucky to get paid to do it. However, there are days when I don't feel as though I'm expressing my calling. Thankfully, I always know that no matter what the day holds, no one chooses what I do from 10 to 12 at night except me. And for at least two hours a day, I can do what brings me the deepest sense of meaning and satisfaction.

"My life has been dramatically altered for the good by ordinary people who spent the edges of their day doing what they felt they were created to do."

It's not negotiable.

Unless lightning is in the area, or a church member is near death, (in other words, unless someone is dying or I could die), I'm playing golf on Friday morning.

Why?

Because if I don't, I'll work.

I love my job, at least most of it.

It's at the core of who I am. Paid or unpaid, I would do what I do. It's one of the reasons I'm happy —I love what I do.

However, even if you love what you do, you can't do it all the time. You weren't created to do so.

We were created to work, but we were created to work around periods of rest. It's the rhythm of life.

We see it modeled for us:

- We inhale and exhale

- The sun rises and sets

- The heart contracts and rests

- We plant and harvest

Life is lived in a rhythm and we were created to submit to that rhythm.

One of the great rhythms of life is work and rest.

Even so, we often ignore this rhythm.

Some ignore it by refusing to work. We were created to work but we are prone to laziness. We have energy, talents, and resources which have been given to us in order to make the world better. Unless we're finding a way to contribute, we will not be happy. Work doesn't have to be something we're paid to do. We were not created to have jobs. We were created to contribute to society. Unless we're using our God-given gifts for the benefit of others, we are operating contrary to how we were created.

Some ignore it by refusing to rest. While many refuse to work, most of the people I'm involved with refuse to rest. We're deceiving ourselves into believing we are more important than we actually are. The world can go on without us. While we are important, we are not indispensable. Not only can we rest, we must. We are not able to operate at a constant pace. We need sleep, rest, a change of pace, and a time to simply "be," instead of always "doing."

Unless we work and rest, we will not experience satisfaction. Resting without work makes us restless. Working without rest makes us exhausted. We must do both.

Do you work?

- Do you regularly use your talents for the well-being of others?
- Are your days regularly filled with work that gives you a sense of satisfaction?
- Is someone or something better because of your contributions?

Do you rest?

- Are there scheduled times of the week set aside for you or your family, which are off-limits to others' expectations?
- Is there something that refreshes you on a weekly basis?
- Is there something you do on a regular basis for no other reason except that you enjoy it?

Look around. Life is lived in rhythm. The process is clear—work and rest. Don't be deceived into thinking you can live outside this rhythm without experiencing negative consequences. This is how we were created. We would be wise to submit to that creation.

Notes

5

Mistakes

One of the most important financial principles is that of compounding. Wise people use this principle with their finances.

Compounding is the simple idea that as money is saved, interest is paid. Yet interest paid this year earns interest the next year. So if you earn 10% on a $100 investment, this year you get 10% on $100, but next year you receive 10% on $110. Over time, the principle of compounding leads to remarkable results.

While many learn about the idea of compounding when it comes to finances, it also has other ramifications.

One of the most important areas of life where compounding works is with bad decisions. Few realize the compounding effect bad decisions have on our lives.

For example, Sarah makes a series of bad decisions when she is in high school. She realizes her mistakes and works hard to correct them. However, as she spends her early twenties correcting the mistakes from her late teens, she often has to delay learning the lessons and skills the average 20-year-old should be learning. This means she may spend her late twenties learning the lessons she should have learned in her early twenties.

Her early mistakes compounded into more trouble. Of course, when she begins to make wise choices, those choices will compound as well. It's amazing how radically different life can be after five to 10 years of wise choices, but it does take time.

One of the most frustrating aspects of the pastorate is to watch people make foolish decisions for ten years, have a moment of clarity and begin to make wise choices only to give up after six months because their lives are not perfect.

You can't walk the wrong way for ten years and expect to be in a good spot after six months.

Because of the nature of compounding and in light of human nature which is prone to make bad decisions, it is vital that we learn one of life's most important lessons:

When something goes wrong, DO NOT MAKE IT WORSE.

This principle will save a lot of heartache.

One of the greatest mistakes we make is to follow a mistake with a mistake. We choose poorly, experience the negative consequences, and then make an even worse decision.

How many rebound relationships compound our original heartache?

How many attempts to get out of debt quickly end up adding to our debt?

Wise people are never perfect, but they do realize when a mistake is made they need to be extra cautious to stop the cycle. Without intention, one bad decision often leads to another and then another. Over time, the bad choices compound.

This is why the old statement, "Sin takes you further than you want to go," is often true. Our bad choices have a compounding effect of negativity on our lives and the lives of others. It is a dangerous reality we must understand.

We all make mistakes. And we will all experience the negative consequences of our decisions. While we can't be perfect, we can recognize bad decisions, admit them, and correct them as soon as possible. When we do this, we limit our bad decisions and prevent them from compounding.

Compounding is an important principle when it comes to our finances, but it is far more important when it comes to decision making.

Choose wisely. And when you don't, do not make it worse.

When life falls apart, don't make it worse.

There are a lot of other things to do or not to do, but the number one rule is don't make it worse.

Life is guaranteed to fall apart. Dreams die; hopes are dashed; expectations go unmet. If your life has never fallen apart, you probably haven't lived long enough. Life will fall apart.

When that happens, the great temptation is to make horrible decisions which unfortunately make a bad situation worse.

- The grieving widow recklessly spends the life insurance money
- The ignored teenager seeks solace from the first boy to give her attention
- The cheated-on spouse finds a fling to even the score

When life falls apart, we make it worse.

We make bad decisions; we do foolish things; we fall into a hole and dig it deeper.

A majority of life's problems are not a result of what happens to us but are a result of our responses to what happens to us.

Generally speaking, we can handle what life throws our way, but we cannot afford to make those situations worse by our own poor decision making. Yet that is exactly what we do.

When something goes wrong, the number one goal should be not making a bad decision, which could make the problem worse. Success in this goal can save a lifetime of turmoil.

Why?

The obvious question is: Why does humanity so often make bad situations worse?

The answer is simple: It's because when life falls apart, we are in no position to make a wise decision.

When your spouse cheats, when your house burns, when you get fired, so many emotions flood your mind that it's nearly impossible to make a wise decision, yet many decisions have to be made.

Instead of realizing our vulnerability, we ignore our need for help and attempt to make good decisions.

Sadly, we don't always make good decisions when life is going good. What gives us the arrogance to think we will make good decisions when life goes bad?

When we are angry, lonely, tired, or grief stricken, we are not in a good mindset to make smart decisions.

It's in these times that we need to:

Slow down. When life falls apart, most people feel an extreme pressure to make important decisions quickly. Rarely do important decisions have to be made quickly. By clarifying what must be decided now and what can be put off until later, we can relieve the self-imposed pressure which might force us into a bad decision. Fast decisions are rarely good decisions. If a decision can be delayed until we are not in shock or grief, it should be postponed.

Seek wisdom. We should be especially distrustful of ourselves in the midst of difficult times. It's in these moments we should be quick to seek the wisdom of others. Remember, this doesn't necessarily mean listening to your friends, but it does mean seeking advice from knowledgeable people.

See tomorrow. When life falls apart, we don't have to do great things. We don't have to learn great lessons. We just need to live to see tomorrow. The shock will wear off, the grief will fade, decisions will be made. It doesn't have to happen now. Focus on enduring and know that when tomorrow comes, or the next day, or the next year, good decisions can be made.

When life falls apart, humanity should have one major goal—don't make it worse. Do that, and you will be miles ahead of nearly every other person you know.

If I could, I would conduct every job interview at a little league game of the applicant's child.

Anyone who blamed the umpire for the outcome of a game would never be employed.

Before you agree to marry someone, attend a game of their favorite sports team. It's okay if they yell at an umpire or don't like a call, but if they blame the umpire for the outcome—run.

Never hire, or marry, someone who blames an umpire for an outcome.

If they wrongly place blame in sports, they will likely do so at work and home.

Humanity loves to place blame. It excuses our failures, justifies our actions, diverts negative attention away from us, and allows us to play our favorite role—that of victim.

Blame is fun.

In 2003, the Chicago Cubs were five outs away from their first World Series appearance since 1945. Leading the Florida Marlins 3–0, a ball was hit in foul territory and the Cubs left fielder went to make a play. As Moises Alou reached to catch the ball, Steve Bartman, a long-time Cub fan, instinctively reached for it as well, interfering with the play and taking away a sure out for the Cubs.

The Marlins went on to score eight runs before the Cubs got the final two outs. The Marlins won the game, and went on to win the World Series.

Chicago blamed Bartman. They blamed a fan.

What's interesting is they didn't blame Alex Gonzalez. Two batters after the Bartman incident, a ground ball was hit to Gonzalez for a simple inning-ending double play. Gonzalez booted the ball and the Cubs haven't been good since.

Clearly, one foul ball did not cause the Cubs to give up eight runs to the Marlins. Obviously, an error by a player was far more important than possible interference by a fan. Without a doubt, one play never determines the outcome.

Yet we blame, because it feels far better than to take personal responsibility.

We love an excuse—bad calls, bad umpires, bad luck—because excuses don't require any change from us.

Blame and don't change. Blame and don't consider what you could've done differently. Blame and don't form a game plan of how to get a different outcome next time. Blame others and feel better about yourself.

There is only one problem with blame—it's useless.

It serves no purpose.

Consider:

How does blaming an official change an outcome? How does it make you more likely to win the next time?

How does blaming the government make life better? How does it cause you to contribute better to society?

Of course it doesn't.

Blame might make us feel better but it doesn't help.

Whether you're hiring an employee or choosing someone to marry, never get into a relationship with someone who loves to blame, because I assure you it will not be long before they blame you.

They will blame you for their failures, mistakes, inabilities, and unhappiness.

Instead of taking responsibility for their lives, actions, and ideas, they will forever look for an excuse, and more often than not that excuse will be you.

You deserve better.

"Humanity loves to place blame. It excuses our failures, justifies our actions, diverts negative attention away from us, and allows us to play our favorite role - that of victim."

Conversely, if you ever find someone who refuses to blame; who finds himself on the bad end of a call, but understands bad calls are a part of the game; who gets a bad break in life, but sees it as an opportunity instead of an eternal hindrance; who takes personal responsibility for his life—hire them, marry them, befriend them... do everything in your power to build a relationship with them, because those people are rare and valuable.

Umpires make bad calls. Parents make mistakes. Bosses choose poorly. Spouses are not perfect. Wise people know this and expect it. They don't let it surprise them or hinder their lives. Those who are looking for an excuse will find one.

It's a whole lot easier to stay out of trouble than to get out of trouble.

Several years ago I was playing in a golf tournament. When my opponent found out I was a preacher he started asking me to pray for his shots. It happened first when I had hit a shot close to the pin and he had a long putt across the green. He yelled, "Hey, preacher, can you pray for my putt?" I said, "I could, but it may not help." He lagged the ball close to the hole and made par.

A few holes later he was once again a long way from the pin and I was close to the hole. He asked if I could pray for him and he lagged the ball near the cup.

On the 17th hole the same scenario repeated itself. I was near the cup and he had a long putt across the length of the green. Right as he was about to putt, he stopped, looked up at me and said, "Why am I the one doing all the praying, but you are always close to the hole?"

I said, "That's simple, you pray on the green, but I pray on the tee box."

It's a whole lot easier to stay out of trouble than to get out of trouble.

We spend far too much time trying to come up with ways to get out of trouble and far too little time trying to consider ways to stay out of trouble.

I watch as couples take years to rebuild marriages that could have stayed strong with small investments of time over the decades.

How much money and resources are spent trying to return a person to health after a lifetime of poor decisions? Imagine if those resources were spent on the front end in planning a wise life.

We can't prevent every bad outcome, but we can prevent many of them. By making wise choices at the beginning, we can save ourselves countless sorrows.

Here are a few steps which will often keep you out of trouble:

Think. Before an important decision, stop to consider the possibilities. It's tragic how often people make important decisions without honestly thinking about the consequences. Imagine the number of foolish decisions which could be prevented with just a few seconds of conscious thought.

Pray. Actually pray. Take an allotted period of time for real prayer instead of just saying you have prayed about it. Listen to God by reading Scriptures relevant to your issue.

Get advice. Seek advice from people who have experienced the issue before. Learn from their mistakes and successes.

Choose wisely. Ask yourself: "Is this a wise choice?" It's amazing how many options that question can eliminate.

Choosing wisely on the front end can save a tremendous amount of effort and energy on the back end. If you can only pray at one spot on a golf hole, always pray on the tee box instead of waiting for the green, because it's a whole lot easier to stay out of trouble than to get out of trouble.

While it's a whole lot easier to stay out of trouble than to get out of trouble, the fact is we all get into trouble. We make mistakes; we ignore sound judgment; we go against everything we know to be right and make horrible decisions.

Life is not so much determined by the mistakes we make as much as how we handle those mistakes. Most life-altering decisions are not a single decision, but a series of choices. They are a mistake followed by a cover-up followed by more mistakes. Anyone can recover from one bad decision, but it's the series of bad decisions that contain the most danger.

Since we will all make mistakes, we need to be prepared for how we'll handle those moments.

Here is what to do right when you've already done wrong:

Admit it. Living in denial can be fun, but it's never useful. Most bad decisions involve deception. The first step toward the right path is found by telling the truth. Admitting a mistake requires humility, which is a prerequisite for overcoming a bad decision.

Get help. Rarely can we solve our problems on our own. We often exaggerate our expertise on a variety of topics. If we were that smart, we probably would not have made the mistake to begin with. If bad decisions have any consequences, they should cause us to question our own decision making process and cause us to rely on others. Of course, we shouldn't just listen to our friends; we should find experts in our specific area and listen to them.

Seek forgiveness. If another person has been hurt by your actions, you should seek their forgiveness. Explain your mistake, take responsibility, do not blame others (especially them), and ask them to forgive you. Do not say "my bad" or just "I'm sorry." Actually say,

"I was wrong. I am sorry. Will you forgive me?" While we cannot force others to forgive us, we can do everything in our power to reconcile a relationship. The rest is up to them.

Make it right. We can never undo the past, but many times we can do some tangible actions in an attempt to right a wrong. We can pay back money, explain the story to others, pay restitution, or take some action which weds activity with words. Attempting to make things right can confirm to you and reveal to others how much you regret your decision and your desire to do better.

Learn from your mistakes. The most valuable, and often the most overlooked, aspect of overcoming a bad decision is taking time to consider why we made it. More important than overcoming a mistake is making sure we don't repeat it. What value is it to overcome a bad decision if we are just going to turn back around and make another bad decision? Nowhere is this more evident than in bad relationships. Far too few people take the time to consider how they got into a bad relationship so that they might not repeat that mistake. A simple process of reflection and assistance from others can help us from repeating our bad decisions.

Mistakes happen. We all make them. The key is to know how to handle them properly and make sure we don't repeat them.

What's the most important lesson you've learned from bad decisions?

If you don't understand how someone can think the way they do, you aren't listening to them.

People make irrational choices rationally. It may not be rational to us, but it is rational to them. It makes sense; it's the most logical conclusion they can assume.

Knowing this process of decision making makes it possible to understand others. We may not agree, but we can understand. With understanding comes empathy and the ability to find common ground.

- Do you understand why your political opponent voted opposite of you?
- Do you see why your boss didn't like your idea?
- Do you have empathy toward your spouse's position even if you disagree?
- Can you comprehend how someone can see the world from a totally different vantage point?

Failing to understand another person's position is not a sign of irrational thought on their part. It is a sign of failure on our part to take the time to listen and comprehend how they came to their conclusion.

The following statements are warning signs that we aren't listening to others:

- "What are they thinking?"
- "They are idiots."
- "I don't understand them."
- "They don't love their country like we do."
- "They aren't as moral as we are."
- "They have no values."

Anytime we find ourselves saying these words, we should stop and make a second attempt at understanding how the other person came to their conclusion.

We don't have to agree with them, but we do owe them the respect of seeking to understand their position.

> With understanding comes empathy; and empathy is far more important than agreement.

Who do you think is irrational? How have you failed to understand them?

They will do you wrong.

No matter how good you are. No matter how kind or loving you act. No matter how perfect your actions seem. Someone at some point will do something to you that you do not deserve.

One of the guarantees of this world is that you will be done wrong.

It might be out of spite.

It might be from revenge.

It might even be from good intentions.

Maybe you will lose your job or your kid won't make the team or you will lose your biggest client.

You will suffer in a way you don't deserve.

When this happens, there is one simple rule:

Don't do wrong when you've been wronged.

When we have been unfairly treated (whether in reality or just our perception) we face tremendous temptation to make bad choices. Anger, hurt, disappointment, frustration, embarrassment, and surprise are all emotions commonly associated with having been wronged. Not a single one leads to better decision-making.

Bad decisions compound any negative event which happens to us.

Two primary reasons we should not do wrong when we've been wronged:

1. **It will make them think they're right.** This isn't the highest of motives, but it speaks to our desire. Whenever we do wrong after we have been wronged, it justifies the actions another has taken against us. Uncertain of what to do, I've taken actions against others only to have their responses prove

my decision. Had they responded differently, I would have second-guessed my actions. The same is true for others. Rarely is someone certain about their actions. Most every action is taken with some doubt. People are still making up their minds about what they have done after they have done it. If you've been done wrong, make someone regret it.

Fired? Respond humbly. Don't burn bridges. Be a good employee for someone else.

Dumped? Act like a lady or a gentleman. Don't talk bad about the person. Become a good girlfriend or boyfriend the next time.

Slandered? Don't slander back. Stand up for truth where possible. Outlast the accusation through good decisions.

When someone responds poorly to something that has happened to them it gives credibility to the original action. Others see the response and assume we deserved to be treated poorly.

2. **It will cause more harm than the original issue.** More important than what it does to others, we should choose wisely based on its effect toward us. We are hindered far more by what we do to ourselves than what others do to us.

Many wrongly conclude their lives are in a bad place because of what someone else did to them. Sometimes it is true. We can suffer greatly from the decisions of others. In the immediate aftermath of someone else injuring us, we can be devastated—abuse, divorce, job loss, victimization from crime, etc.

Yet soon after the negative event, we begin to regain responsibility for our lives. We do not always control what happens to us, but we do always control our response. While the action of the other may have been injurious, rarely does one action by another person define our whole lives.

Far more often, our lives resemble the choices we made in response to life's events rather than the choices others have made toward us.

Whenever we experience an unfair circumstance, we're in great danger of allowing one event to become the catalyst for a series of bad choices. Without deep reflection, an awareness of human tendency, and an intentional process to protect us from ourselves, we will make bad decisions whenever we've been done wrong. Our decisions will feel right, justified, and self-satisfying, but they will not lead to the results we desire.

We must choose a different way.

Don't do wrong when you've been done wrong.

Notes

6

Time

A day will come when my name will not be remembered. Every word spoken and written, every life influenced, and any legacy left will be erased. My guess is it will happen far sooner than I can imagine. It will only take a few generations before my name is no more.

But even before that day, my life's work will quickly diminish.

There have been few people I loved in my life like my grandparents. They have only been gone for a few years, yet I don't think of them every day. I remember them fondly, and at times miss them greatly, but on a day-to-day basis their absence doesn't leave a void. Even with all they did in their nine decades, someone who loved them most only remembers them a few times a week.

As the old song says, "Time marches on."

With or without us, the clock continues to tick and the calendar continues to turn.

If we aren't careful, we can realize this truth about life and come to the wrong conclusion that because life is so fleeting, it doesn't matter what we do. Because everything we accomplish will one day be erased, why do anything?

It's a false conclusion, but one many people draw.

This is the challenge with time. We all live within its context, but if we aren't careful we can be tempted by two misconceptions regarding its true nature. Either misconception leads to dangerous consequences.

Two Misconceptions:

1. Some wrongly believe we have all the time in the world.
This is often the error of youth. Having not lived long enough to understand how quickly time passes, we can underestimate its value. When we believe a resource is unlimited, we don't value an individual unit of that resource. Believing time is without end, we waste the minutes, hours, and days given to us.

2. Some wrongly believe we don't have enough time for it to matter. This is often the error of those who are older. Having experienced how quickly time passes, we can falsely conclude that we don't have enough time to accomplish anything of significance. Even if we do accomplish great things, we see how quickly they're forgotten or erased, and we conclude the effort is not worth it.

Both of these misconceptions miss the truth.

The truth is that most of us have enough time to do things that matter, but have no time to waste.

We have enough time to accomplish things. We can love, build, create, innovate, dream, design, accomplish, and achieve. Great things can happen. Rarely is it too late to do something. Second and third careers are possible. New tricks can be learned even by old dogs. Amazing things can be accomplished in one lifetime.

Still, no one has any time to waste. Life is too fleeting. Time is too precious. At any moment, the gift of life could be taken from us. Because of the brevity of time, we cannot waste a single moment.

I often have the honor of standing at the bedside of those who are dying. One of the common themes of those conversations is how quickly life passes. Whether the person is suffering from cancer in their late twenties or experiencing the failure of multiple organs in their nineties, they look at time in similar ways. It passes quickly.

I've never had a single person on their deathbed reflect on the quick passing of time and think that someone should throw their hands up in apathy and attempt nothing great. Instead, those facing death look at the brevity of life and wish they would have wasted less time and dared to attempt greater things.

We have enough time to do great things, but we don't have a second to waste.

At least admit it—you chose it.

There are times when the pastorate feels completely out of control. There is a set routine to a week—Sunday is always coming. Certain activities must take place whether it's a normal week or I'm sick or on vacation. In addition, the pastorate is often built around crisis ministry. You never know when someone might die, have an affair, or get arrested (and sometimes those three are related). There are moments when I feel I have no control over my life.

But those moments are a lie. It's a human deception and I'm not the only one who falls for it.

Have you ever noticed how many people talk about their schedules as though it's something happening to them? It's like someone held a gun to their head, strapped them into a roller coaster and watched it take off.

There's no doubt that many of our lives feel like a roller coaster. There comes a point when you have no choice but to hold on and hope you survive.

However, there is one important characteristic most people forget—you chose to get on the roller coaster.

Some things we don't control. My kids have very little control over their schedules. For the most part I (and the State) choose that for them. While their control will grow, until they graduate high school, how they spend Monday through Friday from eight to three will not change.

Yet for the rest of us, we choose our schedule.

We get to choose where to work. While our boss might dictate our schedule, we get to choose our boss.

The State might demand certain amounts of education for our children, but we get to choose if we provide that education or if they go to a school. And we choose (or give permission for) every second of their schedule outside school.

We may have little say in how clubs, churches, and organizations schedule their activities, but we're completely in charge of whether or not they participate.

The fact is we choose our schedules.

And here is an important truth: If we choose it, we can change it.

Many live in denial of the control we have because we would rather play the role of victim than have the responsibility of living a different life. We claim we don't control it, so we don't feel bad when we don't change it.

It's nothing but denial.

The fact is we do control it. We choose the lives we live—nearly every second.

Don't like your kids practice schedule? You chose to let them play.

Too many activities hurting your family time? You chose the activities.

Frustrated you never get to attend church? You choose what takes priority.

Tired, weary, exhausted? You choose to sleep or not sleep, to rest or not to rest, to live a life with boundaries or without them.

Just want a vacation? You

"If we choose it, we can change it."

choose how you spend your days off, whether you've saved enough to money to get away, and if you will take a vacation.

We control how we spend our time. And if we're parents, we control how our family spends time.

Time management—life management—begins by admitting one simple truth—you chose this. **Whatever your schedule is today, you chose it.** While we often live in denial of that fact, it is tremendously good news.

If we choose it, we can change it.

What part of your schedule needs to change? How will you make that change?

Would you want your kids to live the schedule your currently have? If not, then how are you modeling what they should do?

I need to write my opening line.

(check email)

What's the best way to draw attention?

(Respond to Facebook message)

I think the topic is of vital importance.

(check Twitter)

(make a phone call)

(check email again)

(see if they have replied to my Facebook response)

I often wonder why I don't get more work done. A better inquiry would be to understand how I ever get any work done.

The modern worker suffers from Work ADHD. In our need to live in a constant state of stimulation, we are unable (or unwilling) to ignore the distractions and accomplish the work that matters most, not only to us, but also to those who pay us to do our jobs.

We are squandering our time and wasting the money our employers are paying us. The result isn't just a lack of productivity, but also a deep level of personal dissatisfaction and corporate frustration.

We aren't doing meaningful work because we aren't accomplishing meaningful tasks, and the result is growing frustration by employees and employers alike.

I don't know many workers who feel they have ample time to do what they're paid to do. (And if someone does feel that way, I doubt they spend time reading articles like this). Most of us feel overworked and overextended, all while underachieving and being underappreciated.

It primarily happens for one reason: We are not intentionally choosing how to spend our time. We're reacting to our work rather than actively choosing what we'll do. And the result is our being overwhelmed by meaningless work without any ability to do what would bring us satisfaction and our employer value.

But it doesn't have to be this way.

We can choose a different path that not only makes us more valuable at work, but will also bring us a tremendous amount of challenge and satisfaction.

It all starts with one step: Before starting your day, plan your day.

Without this step, you will not do meaningful work.

Teachers have lesson plans. Coaches have game schedules, Surgeons know exactly who they will operate on and in what order, for any given day.

So why does the average worker not have a game plan regarding their work day?

For many people who have flexibility regarding their schedule, the only definite plan they have is whatever meetings they're forced to attend, and lunch. While both might be important, neither is vital to accomplishing the truly important work we need to do.

Consider how the average person begins their work day:

1.   Arrive at the office without any plan.

2. Engage in small talk with co-workers.

3. Check email.

4. Begin fighting the most pressing fire of the moment.

Nothing could prevent a productive start to a day more than these four activities. It causes us to begin in a slow, distracted, purposeless manner. When starting the day this way, it's not uncommon for me to be several hours into my workday and realize I haven't accomplished anything.

But what if you chose a different way.

What if you started your day this way:

1. Before you get to work, list the three most important tasks of the day.

2. After arriving, immediately go to your desk and accomplish the first task.

3. Do not check email until at least an hour and a half into your day.

4. After accomplishing your most important task, then consider what pressing issues might deserve your attention.

It might take a day or two for your co-workers to realize you aren't rude. It will take a week or two to break your email addiction so that you aren't checking it every five minutes. However, if you consistently begin your day this way, you will see dramatic results. And if a workplace can create the culture where workers are expected to start their day at a fast and meaningful pace, it can greatly change the working environment.

The worst thing the average person does regarding work is failing to spend their time on purpose. They squander their time to the detriment of themselves and their job.

Choosing with great intention how we do our work will go a long way in changing the work we do.

Are you reading this before work? Take a few minutes to plan your day in light of what needs to be accomplished, what is expected of you, and what this day looks like in the context of the week ahead.

Are you reading this at lunch? Before jumping back into work, consider the afternoon. What are one or two tasks you must accomplish? Do those and then worry about email and all the other pressing issues of the day.

Are you reading this at night? Take a few minutes to plan tomorrow. Make a detailed plan of how you'll attack the next day from the moment you wake up. Place the list on your bathroom mirror, and when the alarm goes off, work your plan.

Imagine it's the Friday before vacation. When you leave the office today, you won't return for two weeks.

What do you do?

Probably the first thing to happen is you find a way to close out the outside world so you can accomplish the most important things. I would shut my office door, close my email program, and turn off my phone. Some things can only be done by me and I would have to give my best time and energy to those things.

Next, you would consider everything needed from you by others. Email would be quickly filtered to find only the most important matters. Paperwork would be largely ignored, except for the most pressing issues.

After the most important work was done and all the tasks that must be completed were finished, you might end your day by cleaning your desk a bit and putting things exactly in place, so that when you return you wouldn't forget what needs to be done.

Have you ever noticed that the day before a vacation is often the most productive? It's amazing the things I can get done in one morning before I leave for vacation–things that sit on my desk for weeks when I'm not leaving on vacation.

There is something about the deadline and the scarcity of hours that offers perspective and ordering of priorities.

Why not work that way every day?

Instead of being lured in by every email and being redirected by every person's minor emergency, why do we not take charge of our schedules every day?

For most, we're willing to take charge of our lives the day before we leave for vacation because we have an excuse. Everyone will understand if we say, "I'm sorry, I'm leaving for vacation tomorrow, so this is what I have to do today."

But without the excuse, we drift into apathy.

We feel the pressure of our workload, but we don't take the necessary steps to control it.

Every email is viewed the same. Every request gets our attention. Doors are left open, phones are left on, and when someone asks if we have a few minutes, we lie and say "yes."

Living like this takes a tremendous toll. Not only are we far less productive, and therefore a less valuable employee, we also feel tremendous guilt and pressure because we have so much to do but so little time to do it.

We feel out of control. We feel that way because we are. But we are because we have given the control of our lives to others.

A vast majority of modern workers could be in complete control of their work schedules, but they give that control to others. Whether through email, drop-in visits, phone calls, or a variety of other means, we sacrifice the most important task for whatever is the most urgent task, as defined by another person. In so doing, we slash our productivity and kill any sense of accomplishment or achievement.

But it doesn't have to be that way.

For many, we can choose how we spend our time. We might have to be in the office at a certain time, but what is done at any given hour is up to us. We should choose wisely.

Instead of reacting to whatever comes our way, we should intentionally do what is most meaningful, productive, and efficient.

How would your life be different if you worked with intention instead of working in reaction to what happens?

What if you worked every day like it was the last day before vacation?

How would you spend today if you were going to be out of the office for the next two weeks?

"How would your life be different if you worked with intention instead of working in reaction to what happens?"

It's a fascinating time to be alive.

If you don't believe that, then you probably aren't paying attention.

Without a doubt, the times in which we live have their challenges.

We seem to be living in a leadership vacuum.

Politics are ugly, personal, and rarely effective.

Many good things that used to be common have become rare.

Yet the challenges of this day aren't that different than the challenges of any time. Today's problems might have a unique nuance, but problems have always existed. The nature of humanity is no better or worse than it's ever been.

But the times in which we live are fascinating.

There has never been a time when educational opportunities have been as available to the average person. While education is not accessible to all, it is accessible to a good number. It is definitely available to every person reading this article. No topic is off limits. Want an Ivy League education? You may not be able to get the diploma, but many classes are online for free or at a very reduced rate. Want to have a meaningful relationship with God? Not only is the Bible available, but an unbelievable number of study resources are also accessible. For many people, ignorance is no longer a result of circumstance but is merely a personal choice. Nearly anything you want to know, you can.

There has never been a time when the average person can make as meaningful a difference in the lives of others. Boundaries are disappearing every day. Yesterday in the mail I received a kind, handwritten note from someone I'd never met, in a town a few thousand miles away from where I live. This person has a physical challenge, which in years past, would have limited communication. But because of technology, he and I can communicate as if we lived near one another, and as though no limitation existed. While power, fame, and money still greatly influence our world, the common person has more influence today than ever. Through social media and technology, we have an opportunity to identify needs, and meet needs, in a way that has never been done before.

The merger of these two factors—opportunity and ability—make this a fascinating time to be alive.

However, when we fail to recognize the gift of living at this time in history, we squander this opportunity.

When we spend more time cursing our days than trying to find ways to contribute to society, we are wasting them.

When we obsess over the faults of others instead of their needs, we are wasting our days.

When we long for what once was (although it probably was never that good), instead of appreciating what now is, we are wasting our days.

Consider: There has never been a better time to be alive, yet a good number of us are wasting this time wishing for something different.

There may not be a greater tragedy than this. The need is great, the opportunity is overwhelming, and we can do something about it.

The greatest threat to making a difference today is a failure to recognize the time in which we live.

One thing is certain—a leader loves the day in which they live. They don't love everything about their times, but they do deeply appreciate the times and the opportunity to do something about it.

Look around. It's a great day to be alive.

Most bad decisions are a failure in timing and not a failure in choice.

Rarely do we choose things which would be a bad choice in every time, circumstance, and situation. In nearly every scenario, when we make a bad decision, we choose an appropriate choice, but at the wrong time.

Consider food. When is the absolute worst time to choose what to eat? The answer is when we're hungry. Dieticians have long noted our poor track record of making bad food choices when hungry. Who hasn't experienced going to the grocery store hungry and coming home with bags full of cookies, chips, and a variety of poor choices? We should only shop when we're full, so that we can make our decisions based on our intellectual choices, rather than what our stomach wants at the moment.

As it is with food, so it is in a variety of other areas:

The last moment you should decide whether to marry someone is when you're having sex as a part of the relationship. The joy of the sex can cause us to overlook issues in the relationship.

Never make a life-altering decision when deep in grief. How many times have you seen the grieving widow or widower waste the life insurance payout in a matter of months because they're making financial decisions in a time of overwhelming sorrow?

Many professionals jump from job to job, not because of career advancement, but because they regularly go through seasons of mild depression. Without reflecting on the timing of the decisions, they fail to see the pattern that every few years they get tired, experience some sadness, and use a new job to break them out of the doldrums.

It's not wrong to get married, spend money, or change jobs. All of us will do those things at some point in our lives. Yet there are times when we should not make the decision to do any of these things. Because we are not in the right state of mind to make a rational, good decision, we should abstain from decision-making.

One of the most important aspects of wise decision-making is being able to identify when one should not make a decision. There are times when we're too tired, too biased, too involved, or too _____ to make a good choice. In those moments, we must either delay the decision or submit our decision-making process to someone we trust.

The difficulty with these moments is two-fold:

1. **It takes a tremendous amount of self-awareness to know we're not in a place to make a wise choice.** Like someone who is drunk and still believes they can drive, we often live our lives in a constant state of weariness, self-absorption, need, or other condition that biases us from making good choices. It takes a good dose of humility and experience to know when we shouldn't be making any decisions.

2. **The choices we make are almost always appropriate choices for some people, or in the right time.** The BAD choices we make COULD be GOOD choices for someone else. It could even be a GOOD choice for us at a different time in our life. If the decisions were clearly wrong in every situation and circumstance, it might be easier. Yet most bad choices are only bad because the timing is wrong.

Back to the food example. It's perfectly acceptable to have a piece of cake. It should be eaten in moderation and within the context of a good diet, but one piece of cake is not a problem. However, when we're starving and we walk to the break room and see a piece of cake, we're not thinking about moderation and a balanced diet. We're thinking we're hungry and the cake looks good. So in the moment, we rationalize. It's just one piece of cake. What's the harm?

There isn't any harm in one piece of cake. But having a piece in the middle of a normal day for no other reason than we didn't eat a proper breakfast is not a good reason to eat cake. And if we continually make choices like that, we will face consequences.

Most of the bad decisions we make are about timing more than choices. Nearly every bad decision would have been a good decision in a different time.

Before making an important decision (Should I marry this person? Which job should I take? Should we move? etc.) make sure you're in a proper position to make a wise choice. If you're angry over some situation, grieving a great loss, weary from illness or lack of sleep, or too involved to make a wise choice, don't make the decision.

Get to a good place emotionally, spiritually, and physically and then make the choice.

"Most of the bad decisions we make are about timing more than choices. Nearly every bad decision would have been a good decision in a different time."

Do you know what today is?

Today is unique. You've never had it before and you will never have it again.

One of the most important aspects about today is knowing what day it is.

My kids are at an age where they play dress-up out of our closet. My son will put on my shoes and hat; my daughter will put on my wife's high heels and scarf. They will saunter around the house pretending to be us.

It's cute when they play dress-up, but it wouldn't be so cute if I did. It's okay for children; it's not okay for adults.

In order to know what we should do today, we need to know what day it is. Not every day is the same.

Based on your chronological age, your responsibilities, and commitments, today is unique. What you should do and how you should live is somewhat dependent on what day it is for you.

One of the most common problems in today's society is people who are not living based on today.

- the 12-year-old girl who dresses as though she's 18
- the married man still living as though he's single
- the elderly woman refusing to realize it's time to give up the car keys

There is a day to dress as though you are 18, or to live as though you are single, or to drive, but there are days you shouldn't.

Foolishness is trying to live today as though it is yesterday or tomorrow.

One of the wisest actions we can take is to consider what day it is and to live according to that day.

Too many people aren't willing to live today. They are still living in yesterday, or are trying to rush tomorrow. Either is a denial of today. Either is foolish.

Wisdom is the ability to understand how today is unique compared to yesterday and tomorrow, and choosing to live today.

For some, today is a day to pay your dues. For others, it's a day to reap what you've sown.

For some, it's a day to ignore your dreams and to stay home to raise kids. For others, it's a day to let nothing stand in the way of your dreams.

For some, it's a day to enjoy being a child and let your parents worry about everything. For others, it's a day to grow up and be your own man.

Failing to live in our proper day can have disastrous consequences.

It destroys families. Men and women refuse the responsibilities of marriage or parenthood and make foolish choices. Their decisions would be fine if they weren't married, or if they didn't have kids, but with a family they are horrific decisions.

It destroys businesses. Too many never change and are shocked when what worked yesterday doesn't work today. Others try to rush growth and extend themselves beyond their resources. Either choice can destroy a company.

It destroys individuals. Living the wrong day causes some to grow up too fast and others to never grow up.

Families, organizations, and individuals all have to ask, **"What day is it?"** before they can figure out the answer to the more prevalent question of, **"What should I do?"**

Take a look around. It's easy to see. Far too many people are not living today. Individuals, businesses, and communities are suffering because of it.

Figure out the day and you will figure out what you should do.

Families, organizations, and individuals all have to ask, "What day is it?" before they can figure out the answer to the more prevalent question of, "What should I do?"

Notes

7

People

Humility knows something pride does not: achievements accomplished together are just as valuable as those accomplished alone.

- Whether you study alone or with a group, if you make an A on the test it's an A.
- Whether you stop smoking cold turkey or do it via medical intervention, you still have stopped smoking.
- Whether the idea was solely yours or was the by-product of group-think, your company still sells the product.

Pride tells us the great lie that it means more if we do it alone. If it is MY idea, MY accomplishment, MY doing from start to finish, the outcome will be better. People will respect me more. The feeling of satisfaction will be deeper. Success will be sweeter.

But it's not.

The outcome is the same, and sometimes the process is lonelier, tougher, and ripe with more peril.

Humility tells the truth: I don't have to do it on my own. Neither do you.

The things that are truly worth doing are worth doing no matter how they are done. Accomplished alone or together, what really matters is that they are accomplished.

Humility knows we can almost always accomplish more together. So it doesn't care who gets credit for the idea. It doesn't need recognition. It doesn't dissect every aspect to give proper due. Humility is more concerned with getting important things done than getting credit for having done something.

Pride prevents more accomplishments than anything else.

- How many marriages stay adrift for decades because one of the spouses has too much pride to ask for help?
- How many careers never reach their potential because the employee feels pressure to go it alone?

- How many addicts continue to act on their addiction because they won't admit they need help?

It's all pride.

Humanity is not very good when left alone. We were created for community, for intimacy. We are complete as individuals but we thrive with others—with families, teams, communities, friends, and collaborators.

Pride warns us to stay by ourselves. It says we should go it alone in order to get all the glory and to fend off any threats from others.

Humility invites us to reveal our inabilities, admit our inadequacies, and to seek help.

What dreams are left unaccomplished? What addictions are still having their way? What projects are stagnant? What personal struggles keep repeating?
Is it time to get help? Is it time to stop trying to do it all by yourself? Is it time to admit you can't figure it out?

Tell yourself the truth. You don't have to do it on your own. Any achievement accomplished with the help of others is just as valuable as one accomplished alone. And it could be that those accomplished together are sweeter because you have someone who knows the struggle it took to experience success.

The only thing we know is that we don't know.

We don't know people's hearts. We don't know their potential. And we don't know what they might do.

Every time I think I have someone figured out, they surprise me.

Sometimes this is bad news.

- The person I think could never fail, fails.
- The confidant I think could never betray, betrays.
- The friend I think will always be there, isn't there.

I know people fail because I fail people. Others are no different than me.

Yet people can also surprise me in very good ways.

- The addict finally comes clean in his 11th rehab.
- The marriage finally experiences a breakthrough.
- The rebellious child finally settles down and grows up.

As disillusioning as people's bad actions can be, there is nothing more inspiring than someone who begins to make consistently good decisions.

We should never give up on people:

1. Because they can always surprise us. The moment we think we have someone figured out, they will often do the opposite of what we expect.

2. Because we never want others to give up on us. No matter what we do, we do not want others to stop believing in us.

Over a decade in the pastorate has taught me to never give up on someone.

This doesn't mean I blindly trust everyone I interact with. It doesn't mean I give unending opportunities to people and allow them to continually disappoint me.

It's possible not to give up on someone but still:

Establish proper boundaries. Some people don't deserve my trust. They have failed to earn it and I will not give it easily.

Ensure you aren't enabling. I can believe in someone but not pay their bills. I can hope for someone to make a wise decision while allowing them to experience the consequences of their decision making. Often times the first step to another's good decision is for me to stop enabling their bad decisions.

Feel freedom to break-off the relationship until they choose differently. I don't think the father of the Prodigal Son ever gave up on him, but the father didn't chase his son to the pig farm. He let him go. He allowed the relationship to be broken without giving up on his son. Just because I refuse to be involved with someone who—is an active addict, refuses to take responsibly for themselves, cannot play an active role in a healthy relationship— does not mean I have given up on them. I still hope for the best, but I will not engage their current lifestyle.

Protect myself and my family. I can hope the best for someone but still take measures to protect myself or my family. I can still have hope for the addict while refusing to allow them to be in the presence of my children. I can expect the best from a former thief while not giving them unattended access to my belongings. Taking appropriate action is not giving up on others.

Even as I do these things, I can still believe, hope for, and expect the best regarding others.

Nothing should surprise us.

In 2008, Mikhail Gorbachev confessed he was a Christian. Upon hearing about it, my first thought went to the moment he dies and shows up in heaven. Imagine the shock of so many Americans who died in the late 1970s and early 1980s. The last person they would've ever expected in heaven was the leader of Soviet Russia. Yet the amazing thing about grace is that it is powerful enough to cover anyone's sins.

It is the Christian story that we should never give up on anyone because God never gave up on us.

Because of this:

I will always pray for someone no matter the circumstances.

I will always communicate the truth if they seek it.

I will always be open to assisting someone if they will take the steps necessary to heal.

It's true of us and it's true for others— never give up on people.

When did it become the norm to dislike people?

Notice it at work–people are quick to name co-workers they don't like, to mock clients or customers, and to demean others.

Notice it among friends–how much conversation is spent degrading people, gossiping, or complaining?

Notice it at church–how much time is spent in Sunday school or in the foyer talking about how people have frustrated us.

Maybe it's always been this way, maybe it hasn't, but the normal thing to do today is to dislike people.

Do you want to be different? Would you like to stand out?

One of the easiest ways to stand out at work, among friends, or in society is to simply like people.

I Like People

There are very few people I struggle to enjoy. I like people.

And it's a good thing.

Being a pastor puts me in contact with a variety of individuals. If I didn't like them, it would be difficult to serve them.

I was playing golf a few years ago with some friends I see regularly and someone I had just met. Throughout the round, different names of people would be mentioned and without realizing it, I kept saying, "He's a good guy," or "I really like him," or "She's very kind." Late in the round, the person I had just met turned to me and asked, "Is there anybody you don't like?"

I thought for a moment and said, "Not really. For the most part, the only people I don't like are the ones I haven't met. There are some people on social media who irritate me, but by and large, if I've met you, I like you."

My new friend couldn't understand it, but I think I know why I tend to enjoy relationships with a variety of people.

3 Steps to Liking People

There are three basic steps to liking every person you meet.

1. **Forgive Quickly.** One of my favorite old songs opens with "Everyone needs compassion." It's true. We all stand in need of forgiveness. Those you don't like are likely those you haven't forgiven. Whenever we are quick to forgive others—not quick to deny mistakes or ignore them, but quick to forgive them—we create a climate where a relationship can take place. Without forgiveness, we will never have the ability to appreciate someone for who they actually are.

2. **Judge solely on personal experience.** Never judge a person based on the experience of another; decide for yourself. Many relationships are tainted before they begin because we have heard how someone acted or treated another. The only problem is that we weren't there. Everything we've been told has been filtered by someone else. While I might use references before I hire someone or go into partnership with them, I will not allow other people to influence whether or not I like a person. I will only judge you based on my personal experience.

3. **Always seek to understand.** The main reason we don't like people is because we don't understand them. We write a story about their lives that is not true. Whenever we seek to understand what motivates another person it helps us to have compassion toward them. If someone ignored you in Walmart, you might think they were a jerk. If someone's mother died and you saw them at Walmart, if they ignored you the assumption would be that they were distracted or grief- stricken. Both situations are the same— they ignored you—but in the first story you assumed they were a jerk and in the second story you assumed they were a

grieving child. Understanding changes everything. Whenever someone does something we don't like, seek to understand why they might have done it. And don't jump to a negative conclusion. Determine some possible reasons and assume the best.

While there may always be an exception to the rule, almost without fail, if you're quick to forgive, judge solely on personal experience, and always seek to understand, it's pretty easy to like people.

And when you like people, you tend to like life.

Attempting to please people is not the same as loving them.

I am a people-pleaser. Many pastors are.

Generally, my attempt to please others expresses itself in kindness, concern, and a willingness to submit my own desires for that of another.

It mimics love. And oftentimes it is love.

But not always.

Sometimes my desire to please people has very little to do with the people I'm trying to please and very much to do with myself. It might appear as if I'm thinking about them, but I'm only thinking about them in reference to me.

- How would this make me look?
- How will they feel about me?
- What will my reputation be?

People-pleasing might appear loving, but it isn't. It's selfishness masquerading as selflessness. It's pride attempting to appear as humility. It's self-centeredness acting like concern.

People-pleasing may be one of the most dangerous activities because it is so easy to convince ourselves we're loving people. We can make a list of the sacrifices we've made for others—forgetting that the very presence of a list shows we've kept a record to prove our sacrifice.

Acting out of a desire to please people is not an act of love because it's using others to form our own sense of identity and satisfaction.

It might appear as love, but it is not love. To love someone is to act in their best interest—no matter how they feel about it.

While I often desire to please people, my actual call is to love people.

The difference:

Pleasing people is doing what they believe is best.

Loving people is doing what is actually best.

If people are always pleased by you, then you are not always loving them. Love is what causes a parent to discipline their child. It forces a boss to tell an employee they might need a different career path. It causes a doctor to give a child a shot.

Love often displeases people. We don't always want what is best for us. We want what is comfortable. When someone makes us comfortable, we are pleased by them. We often find comfort in the pleasure of others.

Love isn't so comfortable.

It can actually be offensive.

Upholding a reasonable boundary with your mother-in-law can offend her.

Compassionately, but honestly, telling the truth can hurt the feelings of others.

Allowing someone to experience the consequences of their decision making can frustrate them.

A people-pleaser would struggle to take any of those actions. Someone acting in love might have to make those exact choices on a regular basis.

> "Pleasing people is doing what they believe is best.
>
> Loving people is doing what is actually best."

Too often, I'm overly concerned with not offending people, but under-concerned about truly loving others.

Love always does what is best for the other person, no matter how that person feels about an action. Love is unmoved by the response and makes a decision solely based on what is best.

People-pleasing always focuses on the response. How will the other person react if I do a certain action? If I like their response, I do the action. If I don't like their response, I don't do the action.

There is a simple distinction between people-pleasing and love:

People-pleasing is always about me.

Love is always about the other.

Which are you about?

Do what is loving.

Nothing defines which action is right as much as those four words.

Always do what is loving. As a pastor, I would define the opposite of love as sin.

Determining the right action in any situation is as simple as finding the action which is most loving.

Our problem is that love doesn't always feel loving. And what feels like love can sometimes be the opposite.

It feels loving to bail out the drug addict for the tenth time and to use your connections to ensure they face no legal ramifications. It feels unloving to let your firstborn sit in jail overnight. But which action is the most loving?

It feels loving to say nothing even though your spouse has used hurtful words. It feels unloving to say how you feel and risk a fight. But which action is the most loving?

It feels loving to give money to the person with the sad story. It feels unloving to turn them away. But which action is the most loving?

Right is not determined by what feels the most loving but by what actually is the most loving.

Feelings can deceive. We must determine which action is loving, not which one feels loving.

Here are a few questions to assist us in finding the most loving action.

How to determine what is loving:

Is it within my right? Just because something is right doesn't mean we have the right to do it. Many times we are wrong to say something to someone, not because what we say is wrong, but because we don't have the right (or relationship) to say it. No matter how right the parenting advice you give a stranger in Walmart, it's probably not a loving action to give such advice because you have not been asked your opinion. If something isn't your business and you don't have the relationship to say something, no matter what you say, it's likely wrong.

Is it in the other person's long-term interest? Probably the greatest distinction between what is loving and what feels loving is the long-term effect of the action. Many things that feel loving don't stand the test of time as a loving act. Many things that feel unloving in the moment are actually in the person's best interest over a long period of time.

Is it within God's boundaries? Love will never violate God's commands. One of the easiest ways to deem an action as unloving is to determine if it violates what God has commanded.

Is it more for them than us? Things that feel loving, but aren't, often feel so because they make us feel good. Love is in the best interest of another, whereas the feeling of love is often in our best interest. Many things disguise themselves as loving because they make us feel good for doing them. It's the ultimate deceit—we feel good for doing what we think is loving even though it's the opposite of love.

Every action—in parenting, leadership, marriage, and life—should be born from love. Love is right, yet knowing what is actually loving isn't as easy as we think. Many things feel loving even though they aren't. Distinguishing between what feels loving and what actually is loving is the first step toward acting wisely.

It was an irritating scenario. The truck was blocking traffic. No one knew what it was doing. The driver didn't seem to care about the inconvenience being created for others. He was blocking the road and everyone else would have to deal with it.

The only saving grace of the whole situation was that being a commercial truck, the name and number of the business was clearly printed for all to see.

And so people began to call. Some were kind and simply asked for the truck to be moved. Some were not so kind and more bluntly told the owner to move the truck. Others were rude, using language not fit for this book.

But what no one was—observant.

No one noticed the driver slumped over the steering wheel. No one realized he needed help. No one came to his rescue.

As a man lay dying inside his truck, the only response from those around were phone calls to the business asking the owner to get the truck out of their way.

This story could be a metaphor for our culture.

There are a lot of people cursing the trucks of this world. Much of it is understandable. Even for those of us with a high irritation tolerance, there are things that are irritating. Few things go as I think they should and a lot of people seem to be doing things I think they shouldn't.

While I shouldn't be irritated about everything, there are many things that rightly deserve my irritation.

Yet, what good does it do? Strangely, my irritation only really bothers me. It might make me less pleasant to be around, but those around me can choose to leave. Unfortunately, I'm stuck with me.

But more important, my irritation is blinding me to the big picture issue—people are dying.

We live in a world where people are dying. If you believe in the Christian message, you believe people are dying. If you trust the words of Jesus, you believe people are dying. If your trust has been placed in God's grace toward you, then you believe those who haven't experienced his grace are dying.

People are dying, but many of us are more concerned with how their death is irritating us rather than the actual fact that they are dying.

While they are struggling in the driver's seat, we are cursing the truck blocking our way.

Doubt it? Check Facebook. Read the negative posts and ask a simple question, "Does this post show compassion toward the person who hasn't experienced God's grace?"

Question it? Go to a public place like a beauty shop or coffee shop where group discussion happens. Are the political rants focused on the issues at hand or are they demonizing people who don't think or vote like us?

Still don't believe it? Listen on Sunday in the foyer of the church or during the fellowship time before Sunday school. How much of the gospel do you hear?

What amazes me about Jesus is that he came to this world but he was very rarely irritated by it. He didn't approve of sin or condone inappropriate choices. He wasn't light on the truth and didn't back away from tough love. Yet He wasn't irritated by the lostness of others; He was compassionate toward it—toward us. Having opened our eyes to grace, I would think He would expect us to be the same way.

Come to think of it, I can only think of one group that irritated Jesus—the religious people who were irritated by everyone else.

We don't live in a perfect world. For the Christian, many things are dishonoring God and should cause great mourning within our hearts.

But there is a bigger issue than the visible effects of sin we see on a daily basis. There are dying people all around us and we have the good news that can bring them alive.

Before we curse the truck, let's make sure we check on the driver.

"What amazes me about Jesus is that he came to this world but he was very rarely irritated by it. He didn't approve of sin or condone inappropriate choices. He wasn't light on the truth and didn't back away from tough love. Yet He wasn't irritated by the lostness of others; He was compassionate toward it—toward us. Having opened our eyes to grace, I would think He would expect us to be the same way."

"I'll scratch your back if you'll scratch mine."

This phrase of reciprocity often makes the world go 'round. None of us can make it through life without the help of others.

It's a way of life I often follow. I shop local before going to national stores. I eat at restaurants owned by friends. I refer others to people I know and like. They help me so I'm quick to help them.

There is nothing wrong with this way of thinking. It is a healthy way to do business and live life.

But what if we removed the second half of the phrase?

Instead of looking for people who can help us and then going out of our way to help them, what if we just helped other people?

What if we lived by a "I'll scratch your back" mentality?

The problem with reciprocity is that if we aren't careful the only reason we give is to get. Service becomes a transactional relationship. We are constantly looking out for ourselves. Even when serving others, we are doing so with ourselves in mind.

This is not the nature of love. A truly loving act is one that is done for the benefit of another without expecting anything in return.

Consider: If the only time I scratch a back is when someone will (or might) scratch mine in return, who am I most likely to help? I help those who are equal or more powerful than me. I help others who I think can help me in return. So for me to help, someone needs to have something I want or some ability I need. I look for what I need and then help with the hopes of getting something back.

It's the way of reciprocity, but it is not the way of love.

Love does not serve others as a means to get something for self. It is not self-seeking because love is not self-seeking. Love so focuses on the object of its affection that it loses all sense of self. Love does not serve to get, but serves to serve.

When every action is for reciprocity, we are not truly loving. We are playing a game of advancement under the guise of sacrifice.

This is not to say reciprocity is inappropriate. It is often wise to scratch someone else's back if they will scratch yours. However, if that's the only reason you ever get out your back scratcher, something is wrong.

Reciprocity should be the exception, not the rule. The rule should be love.

Imagine if we began to serve people without any expectations. What if we went out of our way to serve so that the recipients of our service wouldn't even know whose back they were supposed to scratch in return? What if we assisted others no matter their ability to scratch back? What if we simply met every need we had the power and opportunity to meet, no matter what we got in exchange for our service?

What if we simply scratched every back that itched?

This is the way of love—to scratch every back we can reach no matter if they scratch ours in return.

"Reciprocity should be the exception, not the rule. The rule should be love."

I've never liked the idea that Facebook only has a "like" button. If there has ever been a place that needs a "dislike" button, it's here.

- The political post that's clearly wrong
- The whiny statement from an old classmate
- Anything with cats

If I had founded Facebook there wouldn't be a "like" button, just a "dislike" button.

Yet what if Facebook is right?

What if it's a better social media strategy to only interact with what you like? What if you shared, liked, promoted and interacted with only the things you like?

- No debate
- No rebuttal
- No snippy replies
- No lengthy diatribes

If you like it, interact with it. If you dislike it, ignore it.

What if we moved this strategy beyond Facebook?

What if we tried it with co-workers? Friends? Spouses?

Obviously it can't be a universal scenario. There are times when we must speak about our disagreements. This is no way to raise children. But what if it is a strategy to use more often?

What if I tried to ignore more of my children's minor mistakes? What if I worked harder to highlight their achievements?

There seems to be two benefits to this strategy:

1. **People are more likely to be influenced by the positive than the negative.** When was the last time a Facebook fight

was productive? Has your mind ever been changed? Have you ever walked away from a give-and-take and thought, I'm glad I did that? I doubt it. Generally speaking, social media fights don't change minds. They might sharpen our opinions, but they don't change them. People aren't changed by fights because when we feel attacked, our number one goal is self-protection. Yet, we are changed by positive interactions. When someone interacts in a positive way, we're more likely to open ourselves up to new ideas, differing opinions, and other possibilities.

2. **Training ourselves to see the positive will cause us to see more positive.** Have you ever noticed after you buy a new car that cars with the same make, model, and color are all over the road? Before you bought it, you never saw it, but as soon as you make the purchase, the car is everywhere. Obviously, it's not that everyone runs out and buys the same car as you. What has changed is your perspective. You have trained your eye to see a certain type of car. The great danger with playing the "dislike" game on Facebook, Twitter, social media or any circumstance in life is that it trains us to see the negative. See one negative and it's not hard to find another. See two negatives and the third will appear. See three negatives and the flood gates open. We will see whatever we look for. Look for the negative and you will find it. Seek the positive and it will appear.

Try this for a week. Refuse to fight, respond, or interject your opinions on things that irritate you on social media. Use all your energy to promote things which are positive, important, worthy of your support.

Notes

8

Fear

I know of two main antidotes to fear.

A young friend of mine doesn't want to sleep in his bed these days. If you ask why not, he'll tell you there might be clowns in the closet— not monsters or robbers or even teachers, but clowns.

There has been a rise in self-proclaimed coulrophobiacs over the past twenty years. Most who claim to be afraid of clowns, aren't. It is simply a good way to gain attention—to confess an alleged weakness without really revealing anything personal. I seriously doubt that rapper Sean Combs (P.Diddy) gets cold sweats when he sees a clown, yet he has a "no clown" policy in his contract.

While the fear of clowns might not be realistic, there is something very innocent about a four-year-old that is afraid of clowns. We can identify with him. We can imagine his little eyes peeking out of his covers toward the closet door. We can see his imagination running wild, dreaming of big red shoes, white faces, and multicolored wardrobes masking evil men who seek to do little boys harm. We know too well his fear of being alone with no one to protect him from the clown fury that is surely coming his way.

I'll never forget the last time I needed my father to take away my fear in the middle of the night. In the afternoon my parents rearranged their bedroom furniture. That night I was certain I heard something in the kitchen. I went into my parent's room to wake my dad. He awoke at a far faster pace than I expected. Before I could say anything, he jumped out of bed and ran in the direction of the kitchen. Unfortunately, it was the wrong direction. Before I could get his attention, he had planted his face in sheetrock, which buckled him to his knees.

Of all the times I cried out for my father out of fear, he never did such a good job of taking away my fear as he did that night. From that point on, whenever I heard something that scared me, I'd remember watching the shadow of my father crumble in the darkness, and my fear would be turned to laughter.

We can relate to my young friend not only because we've been in his trembling footed-pajamas, but also because fear is not something saved for four-year-old children in dark rooms. I know it's just as prevalent at every age after that.

His fear is the same as our fears. Yet Unless John Wayne Gacy (serial murderer known as the Killer Clown) lives in his neighborhood, there is no legitimate reason why he should fear clowns, but good luck trying to explain that to him. Instead, his parents will have to be patient.

Chances are, most of our fears are no more legitimate, yet good luck trying to convince us. Our fears feel as real to us as his do to him. Yet when we have fear, I think God sees us in our footed-pajamas and welcomes us into His arms with the hopes of making us feel loved and safe. Showing more patience than any earthly parent, He speaks words of reassurance and comfort:

- "Fear not."
- "I will never leave you nor forsake you."
- "Be still and know that I am God."

There are a thousand different clowns which we can be afraid of today, but we haven't been told to fear any of them. Instead, God continually reminds us that we have no need to be afraid. Fear is not necessary, because God is sovereignly in control. Nothing happens without His divine permission and everything will be used for His glory and our good.

So if you are afraid today, consider either:

- The words of God and release your fear
- Or imagine my dad face-planting himself into sheetrock

One of those thoughts should take away your fear.

An employee resigns and the boss panics...

A marketing plan fizzles and the company is in chaos...

A key family leaves the church and the congregation gets nervous...

Few things cause anxiety as much as change. Just the threat of it can keep someone from sleeping, raise their blood pressure, and cause them to panic.

Yet for others, change is embraced. If things aren't changing fast enough, they might even force change.

What is the difference? Why is the average person afraid of change?

As people who are always changing in a changing world you'd think we'd naturally be adapted to change, or as we age we'd be so conditioned to change that it wouldn't bother us. However, for most people, change is scary.

There seems to be a simple difference between people or organizations that embrace change compared to those who fight it:

Most people are more focused on protecting their current condition rather than striving toward a greater mission.

Without intentional effort, this will be the normal position for humanity. Because the current condition is known, understood, and livable, we seek to maintain it with small improvements. The problem is that we can never maintain the current condition. Change will happen. But when our goal is to maintain the way things are, change is seen as our greatest enemy. It becomes the source of our anxiety.

It doesn't have to be this way. Change can be embraced, even longed for, when we no longer see our current condition as the ultimate goal but instead focus on a greater mission.

I can't tell you why your **business** exists, but I can tell you why our church exists—to bring glory to God by assisting others to follow Jesus.

I don't know why your **marriage** exists, but for me and Jenny, it's to bring glory to God and to be transformed into His likeness.

I don't know why you **parent**, but for us it's to do everything in our power to bring glory to God by making Him known to our children.

The mission is the ultimate pursuit, not the current condition.

Because of this, change is not the enemy. It can actually be a great ally because every change reminds us of the mission and ensures us that each decision is being made with the mission in mind.

Here is the irony: What most people see as their greatest fear is actually their greatest need. Change is necessary because without it we won't realize how much of our energy is being spent on protecting our current condition instead of using our energy to passionately pursue a greater mission.

The sad reality for a majority of people, organizations, businesses, and churches is that we do not have a major mission. There is not a goal beyond the idea of maintaining what currently is.

"What most people see as their greatest fear is actually their greatest need."

Therefore, change is terrifying. It's the only real threat against what we're attempting.

We are afraid of change to the extent that we doubt (or don't know) our mission.

One reason I love the people I pastor is because they have never been afraid of change. From the very beginning they have been so focused on the mission that they have never feared change. The current conditions will always change. We can appreciate them now, but we know they won't be the same tomorrow. Because of this, they are not worth fighting for. Conditions come and go, but accomplishing the mission is worth everything we have.

If that can be true on a corporate level of a church, can't that be true on an individual level as well? Can't we become so engrossed in why God created us, how He did, when He did, where He did, and to whom He did, that we expend every ounce of who we are in trying to accomplish that mission? Can't we do that instead of attempting to maintain something that can never be changed?

Imagine if change was no longer feared. This doesn't mean we embrace whatever happens in life. Sorrows, tragedies, and trying times are guaranteed. However, a vast majority of what creates anxiety shouldn't. The natural changes of life which should excite us, too often create fear.

It doesn't have to be this way.

Find a mission worth pursuing and change will no longer be the great enemy. It will be another avenue pushing you toward accomplishing what is important.

"Can't we become so engrossed in why God created us, how He did, when He did, where He did, and to whom He did, that we expend every ounce of who we are in trying to accomplish that mission?"

The one who screams the most, often believes the least.

Doubt often masks itself in confidence. Insecurity parades in certainty.

When I was a kid, an umpire told me an important concept about being a referee. He said, "When in doubt, pump 'em out."

Years of experience had taught the sage umpire one thing—confidence is important. As an umpire there are two ways to communicate confidence—to have it or fake it. So when the umpire had no doubts about a call, when he was certain a runner was safe or out, he could quietly make the call he knew to be right.

However, when a play was close, when the umpire wasn't certain of what the right call was, he had to exude a confidence he did not have—he had to "pump 'em out." We've all seen it. The bang-bang play that requires a split-second decision by the umpire. He made the simple calls with little flare, but this time, with the crowd roaring, the coaches yelling, he points, with tremendous flare, and shouts, "Ouuuuut."

As it is with umpires, it is with people. We often mask our greatest doubts in outward confidence.

This gives insight into the loudest voices in our lives—they probably believe the least. They are likely attempting to convince themselves and others that they are right.

- The Facebook bully
- The office contrarian
- The obnoxious fan

These who appear the most confident, rarely are.

Confidence most often expresses itself with contentment.

Consider Jesus:

- He allowed the young rich man to reject Him.
- He never raised his voice while others lied about Him at His trials.
- He calmly rebutted the Pharisees when they doubted Him.

This doesn't mean Jesus was without passion. He had no problem yelling at the Temple and over-turning the tables of the money collectors. Jesus was not stoic in nature; He simply didn't have to fake confidence because He didn't doubt what he believed.

Confidence breeds peace. Assurance gives birth to peace.

When one of my children doesn't believe something I say, I don't get angry. I don't yell and scream trying to convince them I'm right. I say what is true and wait. I wait until they experience it for themselves and then when they realize the truth, I'm ready to move forward with them.

Consider the father of the Prodigal son. He knew what was best, but his son couldn't see it. So the father allowed him to go his own way. The father didn't chase him down. He didn't force his way. He allowed his son to experience his mistakes and then the father was ready for the son when the son returned.

Deep belief releases tension. Because we are confident in our opinion, we aren't threatened when others disagree. We feel no need to defend ourselves or to argue the point. We're willing to discuss, but we feel no need to fight. We're happy to share our opinion, but there is little interest in pointless debate.

Doubters debate. Doubters try to prove their point. Doubters seek ways to appear confident.

Understanding this tendency—for unconfident people to try to appear confident—can give us great understanding and empathy for those around us.

- Maybe that person in our office isn't a jerk, but is just uncertain.
- Maybe the arrogant person on Facebook is actually struggling with doubt.
- Maybe the crazed fan is simply masking their own struggles.

This doesn't excuse their approach but it can give us understanding into their actions. Ironically, it causes us to look at them in the complete opposite way we normally would.

When we believe someone is arrogant and they loudly proclaim their opinions, we're tempted to equal their loudness. If we see the person as having great doubts, it can greatly change our approach. Instead of matching their loudness, we can calmly proclaim our point.

Watch a ballgame and notice how an umpire calls an obvious call compared to a close one which could go either way. Then compare the difference to a co-worker, a friend, or a person on Facebook. Assume the calm responses are firm beliefs. Assume the loud or arrogant responses are masking doubt.

FDR said, "The only thing we have to fear is fear itself."

Author Jon Acuff says, we need to "punch fear in the face."

Even I have confessed, "Fear leads me too often."

Fear can be a great enemy to advancement, production, art, and success. Fear can paralyze us, rendering us useless to ourselves, our families, and others.

Many of our fears are built off false assumptions, false beliefs, and false outcomes.

I have little doubt that many fears should be ignored and we should act with great boldness to accomplish our dreams and do meaningful work.

But on occasion, we should be afraid—very afraid.

Fear is not all bad. Much of it is good. It's useful. It's productive. It's reality.

We shouldn't ignore all fear. We shouldn't believe that all fear is a figment of our imaginations.

Many fears should be faced and realized, and our actions should be different because of it.

It is just as dangerous to live recklessly in denial of fear as it is to live apathetically having been paralyzed by fear. Neither action is an appropriate response.

One of the great failures of leaders is not to recognize the fears of those they lead, call attention to them, empathize with them, and assist others through them.

When a leader downplays or ignores rightful fears, they're sending the message that they're either oblivious to what others are feeling or they believe those feelings are wrong. The leader is either ignorant or calloused. Neither is helpful to the relationship between leader and follower.

I would much rather a dental hygienist say, "This might sting," than one who says, "This won't hurt," when it actually will.

By recognizing my emotion and giving it credibility, a leader builds trust with others and empowers them to do what is right in the midst of discomfort. Whenever we propose an action and recognize the fears that request creates, it makes it more likely for others to follow us. The pain actually validates the path the leader has chosen. When a leader lives in denial of those fears, a painful experience can cause someone to question the path the leader has chosen.

Life is full of scary things. Unintended consequences can happen. Bad choices can be made. We can fall victim to the seeming randomness of life through disease, crime, or disaster.

If the only thing we have to fear is fear itself, we don't need insurance, we can ignore medical check-ups, and no one needs Social Security. But, of course, there is much more to fear than just fear itself.

Good leaders recognize the fears of others and they speak to it. They name it; they empathize with it; they reveal that they feel many of the same emotions. But then they come up with an action plan that will help the person move past the fear.

When it comes to fear, we must identify what type of fear we're facing:

Some fear is false. When a fear is false, we must assist a person through the emotions and help them write a proper story.

In freshman speech class, nearly every student is afraid. Much of their fears are false. They are afraid they may freeze, throw-up, or say something stupid. All of those are possible outcomes. However, they also fear the class will laugh at them, mock them, and put them through a horrific hazing experience. These are not likely outcomes. Having taught freshman speech, I've listened to many bad speeches, but I've yet to have a class laugh at a student. When a bad speech happens, the class doesn't laugh, they stop

"Good leaders recognize the fears of others and they speak to it. They name it; they empathize with it; they reveal that they feel many of the same emotions. But then they come up with an action plan that will help the person move past the fear."

looking. They feel so bad for their classmate (usually because they fear making a bad speech themselves) that they stop making eye contact. After the speech no one says anything.

Part of leadership is helping others recognize false fears and replacing them with more likely outcomes.

Some fear is true. When a fear is true, a leader must recognize the emotion, admit the possibilities, and then promote an idea or action that is the most legitimate response to that fear.

When a person faces a serious illness, fear is an understandable feeling. No matter how ready someone believes they are for death, it is still frightening. Many families, and some doctors, are not very gracious toward patients. Because the family or doctor isn't emotionally prepared enough to talk about possible death, they do not let the patient confess their fears of dying. This hinders relationships and treatments. It forces some patients to pretend as though they're feeling perfectly fine even when they are not. It creates a sense of isolation and loneliness. A better way is for everyone to recognize a good or bad outcome are both possible. Depending on the illness and treatment, they may not be equally likely, but they are both possible. By identifying the possibilities and voicing them, families and medical professionals give room for the patient to express their feelings. It helps the patient process what's happening and keeps them from living in either denial or despair.

Part of leadership is helping others recognize true fears and confront them with appropriate responses.

Fear is a real part of life and leadership. A good leader will recognize its presence within the leader, followers, and the community. They will confront false fears with truth and will meet true fears with honesty and courage.

Ignoring fear might be easier in the short-term, but admitting fear and responding properly is a better form of leadership.

Everyone believes there is something holding them back. There is a disadvantage which is keeping them from accomplishing their goals. The prevailing thought is "if only..."

If only I...

- had more time
- would've started earlier
- had a supportive spouse
- didn't have small kids
- had a more flexible job
- could do this full-time
- had wealthier parents

This list is endless. We all assume our goals would be easier to accomplish if something in our lives were different. While it might be true, we often miss the opportunity before us.

What if your excuse was actually your advantage?

I often think it would be much easier to write if I didn't have a day job. Imagine if I could spend all my time writing instead of doing the daily tasks of being a pastor. Phone calls, hospital visits, budgets, staff, and a multitude of other issues seem to take precedence over the next sentence or idea. I think if you removed those obstacles, my production could increase.

Notice a key assumption. I assume if I wasn't having to spend my energy in other areas that I would naturally expend that energy on writing. What I fail to recognize are the benefits the other demands create for my writing.

All these other things:

- give me material
- force discipline
- demand choices

- clear my mind
- get me in the routine of production

With writing being my only task, forcing myself to write would be far more difficult. It is much easier to write when I only know I have a short window and am on a tight deadline. Without fail, I produce more when only given an hour to write on a workday than I do on a cold day off when I have the freedom to write all day long.

What if my common excuse is actually my greatest advantage.

What's true for me in writing is probably true for you about something.

Parents of children with special needs often see the demands of raising their children as the greatest detriment to their marriage. What if it's their greatest opportunity? Caretaking should force them to communicate, demand that they learn to work together, and create a greater appreciation for one another.

It's easy to think that more resources would make success easier, but often those with more don't have the drive or passion necessary to succeed. How many children grow up in affluence only to assume life should be handed to them? Others experience more of a struggle as a child and learn to work hard in order to achieve their goals.

A small organization can compare itself to a larger organization and see all the advantages a larger organization has. They can believe if they were bigger they could do more things. What they don't realize is that in being small, they have a unique advantage to quickly adapt to a changing marketplace.

The difference between success and failure is not the ability to ignore challenges, but the willingness to embrace them. When we recognize the opportunities our circumstances have given us, not only can we confront the difficulties, but we can also find unique ways to leverage our situation for success.

It all begins when we stop making excuses.

"The difference between success and failure is not the ability to ignore challenges, but the willingness to embrace them."

There are few things like the feeling of being on stage, unable to speak, because the laughter of the crowd would drown out anything you might say.

It's an addictive experience.

One that pulls me toward comedy, but I'm not a comedian.

Why not?

The obvious answer is "because I'm not funny." Comedians are funny so I'm not a comedian because I'm not funny. It's a fair argument.

But that's not the reason I'm not a comedian.

It's not my inability to be funny that prevents me from being a comedian; it's my unwillingness to be unfunny that prevents my comedic career.

In his documentary, Comedian Jerry Seinfeld chronicles his return to the road after his sitcom went off the air. Having retired all of his old jokes, Seinfeld worked to create new material. His method—write a joke, crash a local comedy club and try it out, review what worked, rewrite it, find a different local comedy club and try the new material.

Imagine, the funniest comedian of this generation was working on getting five good minutes of material, then ten, and then twenty. In one scene, Seinfeld forgets the setup of his new joke. As he stumbles on stage, someone from the crowd shouts, "Is this your first time?" Even Seinfeld understood the humor in the heckling.

But what amazes me—Seinfeld kept doing it. He continued the process of writing, trying, failing, learning, and re-writing.

He continued because Seinfeld knows what it takes to succeed. Before he could be funny, he had to fail at trying to be funny.

What he was willing to do, I am not.

I refuse to stand on stage telling jokes that do not work. Because of this unwillingness, I am not a comedian.

Obviously, talent, intelligence, and other factors are at play when it comes to who is successful, but none of those things matter if a person is not willing to do what it takes to succeed. Part of what it takes is a willingness to fail.

While I'm unwilling to fail at comedy, I haven't been unwilling to fail at writing or speaking. The thought of standing on stage and telling jokes that do not work makes me nauseous, but I have been willing to stand on stage and give speeches that don't work or to publish articles that do not connect.

Because I'm willing to fail, I have the chance to succeed.

Until you are willing to fail at something, you will never have the chance to succeed.

Until you are willing to have your heart broken, you will never love.

Until you are willing to be rejected, you will never get hired.

Until you are willing to be ignored, you will never speak.

Success requires at least the threat of failure and often the actual experience of multiple failures so that you can learn what is necessary to succeed.

What prevents most people from success is their unwillingness to fail.

Ironically, our greatest fear—failure—is often our greatest need.

We need to fail more so that we will have the opportunity to succeed.

Am I funny enough to be a comedian? Maybe. It's not even a useful question, because I'm not willing to do what it takes to become a comedian—tell jokes that fail.

Thankfully, there are areas where I'm willing to fail. My desire to learn is greater than my fear of failure.

Show me the area where you're willing to fail and I'll show you the area where you'll most likely succeed.

"Until you are willing to fail at something, you will never have the chance to succeed."

Anger is often a tell. It's an outward expression of an inward tension. The inner conflict may be well-hidden even to the person experiencing the tension. Yet the anger reveals something is wrong.

A football coach has an infamous temper. Beyond just the normal driven coach, the stories of his temper become legendary. Finally an affair is revealed.

A good employee who is well-loved suddenly explodes over something so minor it shocks everyone. Eventually a hidden addiction is exposed.

A professional golfer possesses an amazing ability to control every aspect of his life except for an inability to control his tongue after a bad shot. Suddenly the double-life he's living is announced in salacious headlines.

In each situation, highly competent people mastered multiple areas of life, but they were unable to control their anger. Why?

Anger is often a justified emotion. On many occasions I will tell my six-year-old, "I understand that you are upset. You should be. We simply need to talk about the best way to express your anger." When a friend steals his cookie or pushes him on the playground or says hurtful things, it is natural to feel anger. It happens on schoolyard playgrounds and in office complexes, homes, and other areas of human existence. Anger is part of life.

When anger is present in circumstances that should just cause a light frustration or not any emotion at all, the anger is a symptom of a deeper problem.

It often is a sign of tension within a person.

When the person I am perceived to be (or I think I should be) is at dramatic odds with who I actually am (the person few others actually see), tension is created.

> Anger is often like an earthquake. Two plates are pressing against each other and the friction which builds eventually is released in a violent shift. When the plate of perception presses against the plate of reality, something will eventually give. Often the result is a flash of anger.

No one is completely the person they're perceived to be. For better or worse, people write a story about us that is rarely fully accurate.

- The pastor perceived as holy while he's having an affair
- The rich business owner who is drowning in debt
- The well-to-do housewife whose life is falling apart

The tension created by perception and reality often expresses itself with bursts of anger. When someone continually expresses anger in situations where anger is not the proper response, it is evidence there is an internal tension.

We cannot automatically assume the tension is immorality. Grief would be a common cause of displaced anger. A person who has lost a loved one, experienced an illness, or is going through a major life transition could be experiencing grief which can express itself in anger.

We should not use this knowledge to judge others. Seeing an outburst of anger should not cause us to think, I wonder if they're having an affair. Or, I bet they're stealing from their company.

Instead, knowing the common cause of anger, we should experience more empathy, compassion, and understanding.

We should know that anger expressed toward us is rarely actually about us.

As leaders, we should pay close attention to expressions of anger by our employees. It could reveal that we've placed too much expectation upon them, put them in a position where they can't use their strengths, or that private issues are taking place in their lives where they need personal help.

As parents, outbursts of anger from our children could reveal problems that we're not aware of. These outbursts could cause us to pay more attention to their friends, environments, or other signs we might have overlooked.

As friends, seeing those we love suddenly express anger might be a sign we need to ask some personal questions no one else could.

Sometimes anger is justified. When it is expressed, we understand and even applaud it.

At other times, anger is a warning sign. It's an external expression of an internal conflict. If we allow the anger to call our attention to the real issue, it can be a true gift. If we ignore the anger and allow the tension to continue, the consequences will become much more severe than a simple outburst.

Notes

9
Relationships

When everyone knows you're pregnant and is excited for the new addition, word quickly spreads that you're headed for the hospital. When you go to the hospital at the end of an uneventful pregnancy expecting to have a perfectly healthy baby, only to have news you never expected, no one knows how to respond.

Some say the wrong things. "At least..." "It could be worse..."

A few say the right things: "I love you." "I don't know what to say, but I want you to know I care."

Most say nothing.

No one is ill-intended. The "some" are trying to do good; the "most" are trying not to do bad; and the "few" just happened to be more experienced with tragedy than the rest.

When Jenny and I went to the hospital for her to deliver our first child, we never considered leaving the hospital holding a child with a diagnosis. We didn't know how to react and no one around us knew how to react.

As hard as it was, our friends and family needed something from us. Even as they were attempting to love us, assist us, and do everything in their power to help us, they needed us to do something for them.

They needed to know how to treat us.

They didn't know what to do and the only chance for them to learn was for us to teach them.

We didn't greatly know what we needed from them, but we knew some things and we learned many more.

Whenever we go through difficult days—a death, job loss, a diagnosis, divorce, etc.—it's easy to desire and expect those around us to care for us and love us. We all need it at some point.

Yet we know too well what it's like to be on the other side of the equation.

- What do you say when your best friend's wife is cheating on him?
- How do you respond when your son-in-law gets laid off?
- What do you do when a friend's child is accused?
- How do you react when the baby was delivered but there are still no pictures on Facebook the next day?

We don't know. We've all been there. I'm a pastor—an alleged professional in difficult times—and I have no idea what to say or do. I regularly walk toward hospital rooms praying, "Lord, help me not say something stupid." I often put off a phone call because I don't know if the parents of the prisoner want me calling or not.

I deal with tragedy in the lives of others every day, and I don't know what to do. How could I ever expect others to know exactly what to say or do the first time something in my life didn't go exactly as planned.

I couldn't.

So, over the next few weeks Jenny and I attempted to teach others how to treat us. We didn't have to teach their hearts—they were fully desiring to help. We had to instruct what would be useful actions and what would be a waste of time.

For us, it meant:

Don't be afraid to say, "Congratulations" and "I'm sorry." Both communicated what we were feeling.

Be quick to point out aspects of the baby and how she had my ears or her mother's nose.

Ask what we were thinking or what fears we had.

Do whatever you would for any other couple who had a baby–cook a meal, stop by for a short visit, etc.

> More than anything, our friends and family needed permission to act. It was our job to give them that permission.

I'm not saying it's fair; I'm not saying it's right. In a perfect world it would not be necessary. But in the world where we live, people don't know what to do during difficult times. We can either curse the situation and expect everyone to figure it out on their own (and of course they won't, so we will be miserable), or we can accept it and do everything in our power to show them how to treat us (which is actually easier than it sounds and can happen very quickly).

When life hurts, I need one thing from you: I need you to show me how to treat you.

Oftentimes the difference between someone being fully supported through a tough season and someone feeling abandoned is not the love of a community but is the ability of the hurting to teach the community what to do.

When life hurts, kindly, compassionately, and with deep understanding show others how to help you.

At all times we are showing others how they should treat us.

A church member was irate. Something had happened that he did not like and he was voicing his displeasure. There was nothing inappropriate about his opinion or even his anger. He had a right to be mad and, truth be told, I think the actions we had taken were wrong. I was more than prepared to listen to what he had to say, admit our mistakes, and attempt to rectify the situation.

However, as the conversation continued, the church member's anger got the best of him and he began to speak to me in a way no one speaks to me. I'm a pretty level-headed, laid-back guy. While I understand that others have differing personalities, there are some clear boundaries I have drawn. I can take passion in a conversation as long as it's directed at the issue, but I will not allow it to be directed at me.

When the church member began to speak in a more attacking manner, I stopped him, leaned forward and said, "You will not speak to me that way. No one speaks to me that way."

I meant it and he understood it. It wasn't a threat, but it was a clear announcement that unless he changed his tone, our conversation was over.

It would be easy as a pastor to allow people to treat me however they wish. In some cases they are giving large amounts of money to fund what we're trying to accomplish. While I try to give people a wide strike zone, there are some things I simply will not accept. If you cannot treat me with a certain level of humanity, we cannot interact.

In every aspect of life, we are showing other people how to treat us.

Important note: This does not imply that everyone will treat us the way we expect. And in no way am I trying to place blame on anyone who is in an abusive or manipulative relationship. Nor am I claiming they are the cause of it. That just isn't the case.

But it is true that in many situations we have the ability to determine how others will treat us. If we draw clear boundary lines of what is acceptable and unacceptable, communicate those boundaries, and stick with them, others will quickly learn how to best communicate, and how to treat us.

Far too often, we fail to understand our influence within relationships. We think the way people treat us is solely their decision. While they are completely responsible for how they treat us, we can help them understand what we expect, and what would make us end the relationship.

There are two main ways we influence how others treat us.

First, we draw boundaries of what is acceptable and unacceptable behavior.

We are not judging others or pretending to be better than them. We are defining what we will or won't allow. Of course, one of the loudest indicators of the boundaries we have drawn is not what we say, but what we do. Many times, others simply treat us the way we're treating them. We cannot stop others from treating us poorly if we continually treat others poorly. Change how you treat others and that will often change how others treat you.

Second, we show others how to treat us by the way we treat ourselves.

This is often an overlooked aspect of our relationships. I regularly tell single adults, "Don't expect someone else to do what you refuse to do." They expect someone to love them when they refuse to love themselves. I'm not saying you need to be arrogant, but if you don't have basic respect for yourself, why should anyone else respect you? People will often respond to you the way you respond to yourself. Treat yourself better and they might do the same.

Here are two examples of boundaries I have drawn regarding how others will communicate with me:

1. **You are free to talk to me, but you are not free to yell at me.** I'm not a yeller and I don't like to be yelled at. While I give a great deal of latitude in this area, there comes a point where I make my boundary line clear. Someone can yell

about a situation, but I don't respond well when they direct their yelling at me. I figure if my wife doesn't yell at me then neither should you.

2. **You are free to talk with me, but you are not free to talk at me.** I'm not afraid of difficult conversations. I don't particularly enjoy them, but I also don't run from them if they need to take place. But I love the word "conversation." It implies give and take. I understand when someone wants me "just to listen." They desire to be heard and I'm happy to hear them. However, after they have spoken their piece, I expect equal time. To speak at me, but refuse to communicate with me shows a lack of respect for me, my opinion, or my understanding of a situation. It's something I won't accept. We can talk with each other all day long, but if you only want to talk at me, I see no reason for the conversation.

We cannot control every situation and we cannot influence every person in our lives. Sometimes people will treat us however they wish. But oftentimes we have the opportunity to influence them, and on many occasions we at least have the choice of whether we will be in relationship with that person.

Are your children, spouse, friends, or co-workers treating you in a way you don't like? Have you clearly communicated your boundaries and stuck to them? Are they just treating you the way you're treating them?

> "Far too often, we fail to understand our influence within relationships. We think the way people treat us is solely their decision."

The stereotype is of a single woman desperate for a relationship. She's at an age where she assumes she should already be married. It seems as though all her friends are married and having children. She so longs for a relationship that her desperation is felt by everyone around her.

Friends are afraid to even mention a guy.

Her family no longer asks her about men.

Every man she has ever met knows she wants a relationship.

Her desperation is the single greatest hindrance to her having an actual relationship. Anytime someone shows the least bit of interest she smothers them and causes them to flee.

She thinks she's simply being open and trusting. She might even say, "What is wrong with men today? They don't want a real relationship." What she doesn't realize is that no one wants a relationship with someone who would be an open book on the first date.

Trust Should Take Time

Imagine a friend leaving her credit card on her windshield with the password attached via a Post-it note. When you ask your friend about her foolishness, she says, "I'm just a very open person, and I quickly trust people." It would be ridiculous. Yet how many times have you heard, "I'm just a very open person in relationships."

It's not openness; it's foolishness. It's not transparency; it's desperation. It's not the pathway to a relationship; it's the prevention of a relationship.

Openness, transparency, and trust are vital elements of a healthy relationship. However, no relationship should begin with one person immediately giving total access to their heart.

Trust must be built. When someone jumps into a relationship thinking about forever and completely gives the other person access to their heart, body, and soul, they're actually revealing they struggle with establishing proper boundaries and should not be trusted.

> When a guy or a girl feels smothered after the first date or two, they should run because the other person is not in a healthy place to have a true relationship. Because they are in love with the idea of love, they cannot love another person.

The stereotype is that of a woman who falls into this pattern, but it happens just as much with men.

Two False Relationships

There are two current trends within dating that are hindering meaningful relationships.

Some engage in the "hook-up" culture. Refusing to take the risk and be known, they pretend they are above typical dating. They "hang out" and are "just friends," but also engage in serious physical relationships with the very people they refuse to get to know on an intellectual level. Few things will sabotage the potential of a meaningful relationship like ignoring proper physical boundaries. By engaging the body before the mind, we confuse both. The mind can't fairly evaluate the other person as a potential mate, and the body becomes trained to move on to the next relationship when the physical contact loses some of its excitement.

Others are married at the first date. In a culture which is largely rejecting of exclusive relationships, some are creating them well before they should. Desperate for a relationship, they assume if the first date goes well that the other person should be fully committed. This, too, is a recipe for disaster. In no other scenario do we so quickly commit to something, yet some start thinking about forever just because a dinner and a movie went well.

Both scenarios are wrong because neither values the other person. In both cases, the relationship is a vehicle to meet personal needs.

A relationship is supposed to be about another person. It grows slowly in trust and comfort so that we can share the fullness of who we are. This should never happen quickly. It's something that should be earned over time.

We should value ourselves enough so that we aren't willing to give complete access to our heart to just anyone. We should understand boundaries in order to protect ourselves and others. We should not confuse foolishly rushing a relationship with what it means to be open, loving, and honest. We should value privacy and understand that some things should be saved for very few people.

This doesn't mean we should run from love or that we should be afraid to let our guard down. We should, however, wisely progress in a relationship, learning if the other person is trustworthy and kind enough for us to open our hearts.

Many people are more in love with the idea of love than they are with any specific person. As long as they desire a relationship more than a specific person, they will likely experience neither.

I'm sorry to break the news to you, but friends come and go. I wish it wasn't the case. I know it can be painful, but it is the nature of life. Siblings last a lifetime. Spouses come with vows. And a few friends endure from first grade to the nursing home.

Most friendships are not long-lasting. They come and they go and there is little we can, or should, do about it.

It's often said that half of all your friendships will be different in seven years. This isn't a statistic like childhood obesity rates where the stat should scare us into action. This is a statistic that should cause us to give grace to ourselves and to others, as some friendships slowly drift apart.

Friendship is founded on shared experience.

Chances are, most people can remember their friend from first grade. Within a day or two of enduring the new experience of school desks, lunchroom policies, and recess, we naturally gravitate toward people who are like us and experiencing the same things as us. Through the shared experience, friendships are formed.

Yet as those experiences change, so do our relationships. The other day I saw where one of my earliest friends had become a father. As I looked at the pictures on social media, I felt a warm sense of gratitude for him and his family. But I didn't write a note. I didn't make a phone call. I watched online, felt good for him, and did nothing. I don't remember the last time we spoke. I doubt it has been since high school, and it may not have been since elementary school. We were close friends for a few years, but as we grew and were in different classes and then different schools, the friendship began to fade. It's neither his fault nor mine. It's life.

While some friendships endure the changes and become lifelong relationships, most do not. And that is more than acceptable. There is no moral obligation to stay in close contact with every person we become friends with. It would be impossible. While we should always love one another and do the best for and towards others, we should not feel guilt because a best friend becomes just another friend or just another friend becomes someone we used to know. It's just the way things happen.

However, some people who don't understand the ebb and flow of relationships, wrongly conclude that when friendships fade, someone has done wrong. They believe a fading friendship is the sign of selfishness, or a lack of caring, or a rejection. While it could be any of those things, far more often it is only a change in life setting.

An inseparable group of friends are separable when one person in the group gets a boyfriend.

Couples who vacation together every summer probably stop when one of them has a child.

Friendships born in the stands tend to last for as long as the kids keep playing the sport.

No one consciously chooses to end the friendship. And the friendship doesn't actually end, but it does change. The circumstances that brought us together often change, which cause us to grow apart.

It's difficult to embrace this reality. When we feel very close to another person, it's painful to watch a friendship drift away. But there's no need to guilt another person or question our own loyalty when this happens.

Certain relationships must be maintained. We promise to keep our spouse close throughout the changes of life. We hope to keep a healthy relationship with parents, children, and siblings, as life changes. With all these demands, we must give ourselves and others permission to allow some friendships to come and go.

Recognizing this will cause us to have a deeper gratitude for lifelong friendships. It will allow us to look back on past friendships with sincere fondness. And it will give us a greater appreciation for those who are in our lives today, realizing that they may not be there tomorrow.

Most friendships are temporary. Enjoy the time, but accept that the relationship will likely change.

"Most friendships are temporary. Enjoy the time, but accept that the relationship will likely change."

Nearly every relationship problem is a communication problem.

In the simplest of forms, most marriages struggle with three issues: sex, money, and communication. But most of the time, struggles with sex and money are present because a couple cannot communicate about the issue.

Warning: If there is an aspect of sex you cannot discuss with your spouse—that's a problem.

Warning: If you and your spouse can't have a rational discussion about income or expenses—there's a problem.

Most problems are communication problems because most problems can be solved if we can find a way to communicate about them.

There is a solution. A simple solution.

Most relationship problems can be solved by taking two steps:

1. **Ask Humbly.** It requires courage and trust. For many, it's an action that goes against their normal way of approaching things. Many people have backgrounds where nothing is asked directly. Issues are hinted about or implied. Passive-aggressiveness is the norm. Some will even say, "If they really loved me, I shouldn't have to ask."

   But instead of living in the "should be" world, we should live in the world that is. Reality says we never know everything we should, and each of us needs help in understanding what the other is thinking.

   The secret is to ask. Without pretense or anger, state whatever issues are at hand.

We must ask humbly. We must ask about an issue without demanding a specific answer. We must ask to understand how a person feels about the issue. We must ask to get their perspective.

The presence of humility is expressed:

- in tone. Humility is never harsh. It's never cutting. It has a softness and openness about it.
- in content. Humility never assumes to know everything, but seeks understanding.
- in attitude. Humility is the antidote to contempt.

When we ask humbly, we're honoring the other person and recognizing their contribution to the relationship. It provides an opportunity for a solution and seeks help for something we're struggling with.

2. **Answer Honestly.** This, too, requires courage and trust. Far too many people have been conditioned to never fully answer a question. We give partial answers, pretend nothing's wrong or withhold our true feelings.

When we fail to answer honestly, we're hiding. We're failing to disclose our true selves either out of a fear of rejection or because we don't believe the other person deserves to know us completely.

We owe it to ourselves and others to answer questions honestly.

This requires that we:

- share our true feelings. We can't hide or deny them. We must recognize what we're feeling and share it.

- communicate our ideas. Without apology or hesitation, we can share what we believe to be right.

When we answer honestly, we honor the other person by showing them our true selves. It reveals that we're fully engaged in the relationship and are willing to do whatever it takes to solve an issue.

Most problems within relationships are communication problems. By following these two steps, we can solve a majority of the issues which are causing friction.

Opinions come naturally. Without thought, we evaluate a situation and form a conclusion. It's a helpful process that allows us to navigate a complex world.

Many opinions dictate what we do. Without them we would be paralyzed.

Some opinions are just that. They mean nothing and do nothing.

However there is one aspect we rarely consider.

An old friend called the other day, and as we caught up on each other's lives, he told me about something he was doing. Immediately I found myself forming an opinion. It wasn't negative or judgmental. It was just an opinion.

It seems innocent, but is it necessary?

Or is there a better way?

What if we weren't so quick to form opinions? What if we intentionally recognized that an opinion isn't necessary?

As much as I like to think my opinions are innocent, they really aren't.

Whenever I form an opinion, it biases how I view a situation.

If I'm against something and it goes the way I expect, the opinion lessens my compassion for the individual. When I'm against my friend's relationship, I'm less compassionate if they break up.

If I'm for something and the situation doesn't go as I thought, I blame the other person. When my boss agrees with my course of action, I assume he poorly implemented it if it doesn't go as planned.

The habit of forming an opinion hinders my ability to support a friend. Instead of focusing on them, my opinion causes me to focus on me. Everything is viewed through my opinion and every action is dictated by my opinion.

Forming an opinion about everything leads to believing the world needs my opinions. It makes me believe I must judge everything. It causes me to view everyone in my life as being inside or outside what I think is right.

It's not just unnecessary; it is wrong.

By refusing to form so many opinions, I can:

1. Experience tremendous freedom in my personal life. Evaluating every scenario as right or wrong can be exhausting. This is necessary in some situations, but it is unnecessary in most. If a situation isn't my business, why should I care? It profits me far more to spend time on issues that are under my control than to be sidetracked by issues that aren't important.

2. Be a more effective friend to others. My friends don't need my judgment; they need my love. Everyone has decisions that are theirs and theirs alone. If asked, I can assist in the decision-making process, but if not asked, there's no need for me to spend time considering the options.

Consider the number of questions we don't have to answer when we stop forming opinions about everything:

- Whose side should I take in the divorce?
- Do I agree with her taking the job?
- Why do they drive that car?
- Is her wardrobe appropriate?
- Should he spend so much money on a house?
- Should they let their kids play so many sports?
- Do I like her voice? Hair? Attitude?

It's an ingrained habit to form opinions about everything. Most probably occur without us even realizing we've made them. Whenever you find yourself forming an opinion about something, ask two questions:

1. Is it important for me to have an opinion about this? (Rarely is an opinion necessary.)
2. Could my opinion actually hurt the situation? (Often our opinion can have a negative impact.)

Seldom do I have the ability to stop the opinion-forming process before it begins. I see something, and I start evaluating it. With just a little time I can have a fully-formed opinion. But before the process is over I often stop myself. I'm reminded that my opinion isn't necessary and it would be more helpful not to have one.

In my opinion, you don't need so many opinions.

"Forming an opinion about everything leads to believing the world needs my opinions. It makes me believe I must judge everything. It causes me to view everyone in my life as being inside or outside what I think is right.

It's not just unnecessary; it's wrong."

Notes

10

Control

It is a universal feeling to believe you feel like no one has ever felt before.

Remember the first time you really talked to someone of the opposite sex at length. For my generation it was late at night on the phone. For today's generation it might be late at night through Instagram or SnapChat. Either way, the base feeling is the same—the communication stops and you think no one has ever felt this way before.

Of course, the truth is that everyone has felt this way before.

Feelings of uniqueness are universal.

The good news is that:

Whenever you feel most alone, you probably aren't alone.

Whenever you feel the most misunderstood, there are probably many people who know exactly how you feel.

Whenever you think no one is going through what you are going through, there is probably someone very close to you going through the same thing.

While the feeling of uniqueness is universal, it can harbor a great danger.

When we assume no one has ever felt what we're feeling, we can quickly conclude something is uniquely wrong with us.

Good news—rarely is something uniquely wrong with you.

On a regular basis I will listen to someone going through a difficult time. They will express what they are feeling. And almost without fail they all say the same thing.

Yet not knowing they are normal, they draw the dangerous conclusion that they are uniquely messed up. This can have disastrous consequences.

"The danger of thinking we are unique is that it might prevent us from reaching out, getting help, communicating our emotions, or asking if anyone else has ever felt this way before."

- A wrist can be slit.
- A marriage can be ended.
- An addiction can remain hidden.

All because they assume no one else will understand, or they believe that if anyone finds out, they will be ostracized.

The danger of thinking we are unique is that it might prevent us from reaching out, getting help, communicating our emotions, or asking if anyone else has ever felt this way before.

One of my favorite moments when working with people is to match them up with someone going through a similar issue. I love it when two people begin to share experiences and suddenly they realize and often say, "I am not alone."

They aren't alone. You aren't alone.

This might be bad news for some, but it's the truth—we really aren't that unique. While there might be some minor differences in each one of us, our general make-up is the same. We may not struggle with exactly the same thing, but we all struggle. We might not feel in identical ways about the same issues, but different issues do create similar feelings within all of us.

We really aren't that unique, and in the end, that is great news. It means we are never alone; we are never beyond hope. And help is often closer than we realize.

Whatever you're feeling, so is someone else. Wherever you are, you are not alone. The bad news is that no one will know it until someone has the courage to say it.

Be that someone.

Reach out.

Be honest.

Tell someone how you feel and what you think.

But don't be surprised when they tell you they feel exactly the same way.

It's a common question I receive, "How do you write five blog posts a week?" I always answer, "I don't. I write seven or eight a week and from that I might have five I can publish."

Posting five times a week is too much, especially when the average post is 750 words. Generally speaking, a person should only publish a few thousand words a week, not 3,500–4,000.

However, building an audience and a blog is a secondary goal, but my primary goal is learning to write and building a library of information on certain topics. I write for myself—to learn, think, and engage. A byproduct is that others get to read, interact, and maybe be bettered by the words they read. But I've found something to be true since I started—I always have an excuse not to write.

- sick kids
- busy schedules
- dying church members
- late night meetings
- vacations
- work expectations
- family needs

No matter the day, there is always a reason I can justify not writing. Some of the reasons are clearly just excuses, but many are legitimate.

Early in the process, I came home from work to eat and put the kids to bed but needed to go back to work. After returning home, much later, my wife asked me if I was coming to bed. I said, "No, I haven't written anything today." She said, "Just come to bed and forget about it. You can always write tomorrow." It was great advice, but it wasn't the advice I needed. I told her, "I don't need you to talk me out of writing; I need you to talk me into writing."

Whenever I start to make an excuse, encourage me and send me to my desk."

I always have an excuse not to write. If I start allowing every excuse to prevent me from working, I will never accomplish what I desire.

What's true of writing is true of life.

You always have an excuse.

No matter what it is you are trying to do, you always have an excuse not to do it.

- Exercise
- Apologize
- Work
- Rest
- Write
- Invent
- Go to church
- Invest
- Improve your marriage
- Teach your kid

No matter the task, there is always an excuse not to do it. The difference between those who accomplish things and those who do not is most often defined by what we do with excuses. Those that obey them feel justified but do nothing. Those who ignore them can do great things.

I have a friend who is a wonderful musician. After shows and concerts people come up to him and compliment his guitar-playing. Nearly every night he hears, "I always wanted to play the guitar."

When my friend hears this, he often says to himself, "No you don't." Because if they did, they would practice. He thinks back to all the hours he spent practicing and the things he chose to miss out on in order to play, and he knows—if they really wanted to play the guitar, they would've played the guitar.

As I write, it's 11:45 on a Friday night. My kids have been in bed for a few hours. My wife went to bed an hour ago. But I'm on the couch with laptop in my lap. There are plenty of excuses not to write at this moment—I've written a good amount this week, it's almost the weekend, it's late, no one will know if I don't write. I could just relax; my blog posts for next week are already done. There are plenty of excuses, but I'm writing anyway. I'm writing because I know if I begin to listen to one excuse, I will likely listen to them all.

You always have an excuse not to do whatever it is you want to do. Ignore the excuse and do the work.

Comfort or success?

That's the question.

Every successful person I know has one thing in common: they value success more than comfort.

The two are always at odds. You can't have success if comfort is your highest pursuit.

Success demands discomfort.

It requires us to face challenges, to explore areas outside of our expertise, to identify and improve our flaws, to confront others, to face our darkest fears, and to tackle whatever stands between us and success. Discomfort is a consistent hurdle on the track of success. We have to confront it over and over again.

Yet most people are not willing to face the discomfort which success demands.

We won't face it because we desire comfort more than success.

Without intention, humanity will value comfort over all other things. It's why we avoid conversations, deny our flaws, keep making the same New Year's resolutions every January, experience a mediocre marriage, never move up in our career, and have the same hopes and desires as we did a year ago.

Most of us never succeed because we do not have a high enough pain tolerance to experience success.

Consider it:

Does our country have a high enough pain tolerance to suffer through some tough years in order to tackle our national debt or will we keep pushing the debt onto our children and grandchildren?

Do married couples have a high enough pain tolerance to deal with the real issues of their marriage or will they live another day denying the deep hurts and bad habits that are destroying their relationships?

Will you have a high enough pain tolerance to explore the real issues that are holding you back in life?

Without a high pain tolerance, success cannot be found.

Most of us never succeed because we have a low pain tolerance. We value comfort more than success.

> Sadly, when we pursue comfort at the expense of success we end up with neither.

It's the great irony of pursuing comfort; we never find it. We might experience it in the moment, but it's never lasting. Comfort is a mirage which woos us from doing what is right. We ignore the long-term need for the sake of temporary ease.

Yet the constant pursuit of comfort is, in fact, discomforting. The fear of being uncomfortable becomes the most prevalent anxiety in our lives.

How many of our actions are determined not by what is right or necessary, but by what will most likely lead to the greatest amount of immediate comfort.

This is why so many **families are in debt**. They are unwilling to suffer in the moment in order to have financial freedom years from now.

This is why so many **non-profits are dying**. They are unwilling to take action because it might offend a long-term donor.

This is why so many **leaders are failing**. They are unwilling to do what is right for fear they may be disliked.

This is so many **individuals are unhappy**. They are not willing to suffer a little today in order to experience success tomorrow.

Many people never succeed because they value comfort over success. Their pain tolerance is so low that they will do anything to avoid pain. And in avoiding pain, they avoid the only avenue in which success can be found.

Marriage counseling is uncomfortable.

Saying "I'm sorry" is uncomfortable.

Asking others to tell you your weaknesses is uncomfortable.

Confronting the brutal facts is uncomfortable.

Yet it's only in facing the uncomfortable things that we can have an opportunity to experience a successful marriage, career, or life.

Every successful person I know values success more than comfort.

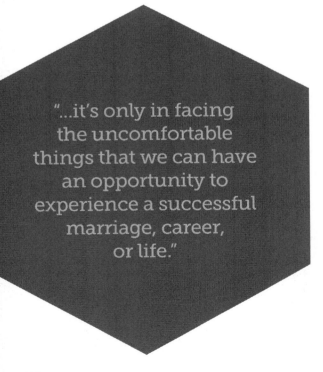

"...it's only in facing the uncomfortable things that we can have an opportunity to experience a successful marriage, career, or life."

What you think is your problem, may not be your problem.

Everybody has something—weight, height, background, something. Whenever you look in the mirror or walk into a crowd, there is something that causes you to pause, doubt, and question.

NBC's *The Voice* attempts to level the playing field so each contestant is judged by the same standard. With each person singing to the judges' backs, everyone is evaluated by the same thing—their voice. Whether she is a size two or a size 12 doesn't matter. Whether he is 18 or 48 isn't a criteria. Whether she is picture-perfect or he is rough around the edges, the only thing that matters is the voice.

What I find most interesting about the show is when someone is rejected and they are shocked. You can tell by the look on their faces—they thought they were being held back by something other than their voice. It was their height or weight or imperfect ears or weird nose or awkward social skills or _____ (whatever fills in the blank). The story they have told themselves is that if they could ever just be judged on their voice, everyone would see their ability.

Yet when the opportunity comes, they don't get chosen. If they're being honest with themselves, they'll realize that what they thought was holding them back really wasn't.

Humanity is quick to make excuses. Instead of taking personal responsibility for our actions and abilities, we look for another reason that things aren't going our way. And sometimes that is the case. Racism, sexism, bigotry, and a hundred other biases result in negative outcomes all the time. But sometimes they don't.

In many situations, what we think is holding us back really isn't holding us back.

The danger in quickly assuming something other than our ability is keeping us from success is that we stop working, improving, and striving. We focus on what we can't change and stop working on what we can change. This is a risky gamble.

What if we're wrong?

What if it's not your looks or your background or insecurity that is holding you back? What if it is your skill?

That's good news, but it's also difficult news.

It's good because you can work on your skill. You can practice and perfect. You seek advisors and experts.

It's difficult because it requires you to admit you haven't arrived. You aren't there yet.

Excuses are easier. If you get skipped over for the promotion because you didn't have the right last name, nothing is required of you. But if you got skipped over for the promotion because you weren't good enough, you now have to figure out how to be better. You have to show humility, admit weaknesses, and get better.

On a weekly basis, I speak with people experiencing disappointment. I'm reminded of how quickly we all run to excuses of why life is not going the way we want. Sometimes it's true, but most of the time it's not.

For a good number of us, what we think is our greatest problem isn't really our problem; it's our excuse.

Stop making excuses. Stop blaming your weight, looks, lack of name recognition, or anything else that is beyond your control and simply get better. Do more. Practice more. Work harder.

Chances are, what you think is your problem is not your problem. And that is good news if you're willing to do the work to get better.

"The danger in quickly assuming something other than our ability is keeping us from success is that we stop working, improving, and striving."

What does it mean to be emotionally healthy?

When someone is physically healthy, we assume the person's body is operating as it should. Health doesn't demand perfection, but it does mean the body can endure normal life with a significant level of success.

The same is true for emotional health.

An emotionally healthy person can properly navigate the demands and circumstances of their lives in a proper and successful manner. It doesn't mean they will be perfect in every situation but it does mean that even when mistakes are made, there are the proper checks and balances to get them back on course.

This isn't a comprehensive list, but consider the following questions to see if you are emotionally healthy:

1. **Do you take responsibility for your actions?** Many people do not. They blame others, make excuses, and play the role of the victim. Emotionally healthy people understand what they control and what they do not. They see more of their life under their control than beyond it.

2. **Can you clearly communicate what you think and feel?** No need to hide or excuse or downplay your thoughts or emotions. Emotionally healthy people have the ability to identify their emotions and properly communicate them to others. If you know an emotionally healthy person, you do not have to read their minds to know what they're thinking. They can properly share their thoughts and opinions.

3. **Can you appreciate people who are different than you?** One sign of someone who is not emotionally healthy is fear.

They are afraid of others and few things are more fearful than differences. Emotionally unhealthy people see differences as problems and cannot tolerate others who think, act, or believe differently. Emotionally healthy people appreciate the differences in life. They understand that issues are often nuanced and other people might come to a different conclusion than them.

4. **Are you defined by other people?** Emotionally healthy people are self-regulated. Their happiness and satisfaction is defined by their own choices and decisions. Emotionally unhealthy people are often defined by others. If someone disapproves of them, they are devastated. If someone makes a decision different than what they would make, they are shocked.

5. **Do you refuse to manipulate or be manipulated by others?** Emotional health is often determined by one's ability to draw boundaries. There is a distinct line between what is my responsibility and what is your responsibility. I respect your boundaries and I do not let you cross mine. An absence of emotional health is often a byproduct of a blurring of boundary lines.

6. **Do you feel emotions without being defined by them?** Emotional health is not stoicism. We are emotional people and must be able to identify, define, and communicate what we are feeling. However, we cannot be fully dictated by our emotions. Part of maturity is the ability to delay satisfaction or to understand that satisfying current desires is not always the best course of action.

7. **Do you make wise choices?** Emotionally healthy people have the ability to do the right thing. Because they are not defined by their emotions or circumstances, they are not rash or revengeful. They have the ability to separate their emotions from their actions and make the proper choices. If a person regularly makes wrong choices, they are likely suffering from a lack of emotional health.

Nobody is completely healthy emotionally. Everyone fails at one or all of the preceding questions. Yet some are better than others and wise people are always trying to grow toward emotional health.

If a few of these questions raised issues within your life, get with a friend and discuss areas you want to improve.

If most of these questions identified problems in your life, call a professional counselor and work your way toward emotional health.

You have more influence than you realize.

Even when you don't know what to say or do, you have influence.

We understand the power of presence in negative terms.

A police officer sitting on the side of the road can make even a slow driver hit their breaks.

A shadowy figure standing in the darkness outside a bedroom window would make anyone jump.

If Bono, lead singer for the band U2, sat beside you on a plane, you would naturally get nervous.

It's been twenty years since I graduated high school, but I still sit up a little straighter when my high school principal is around.

We know other people can influence us even without saying or doing anything. Just their physical presence changes how we think or act.

When I was in college, I played in a golf tournament in my hometown. In the first round, my dad came to watch me play. On the front nine I played horribly. He left. On the back nine I shot three under. As I shook hands with my playing partners, an older gentleman made a wise observation. He said, "Son, whenever you can play like that in front of your dad, you will be able to play like that in front of anyone."

We understand the negative power of presence. Yet what we fail to remember is the positive power of presence. Just our physical presence can calm, encourage, and motivate. Even when we don't know what to say or do. Even when we would rather avoid a situation. Even when we think we are useless. Just being present makes a difference.

When we don't know what to do, one thing we can often do is simply show up.

Showing up is often more important than what we do after we show up.

It makes a difference in several areas:

Marriage. You must be physically and emotionally present in your marriage. It's not just "the thought that counts." Sometimes, it doesn't matter what you're thinking if you're not physically present.

Parenting. Our kids need us. We don't have to go to every game, but we better go to most of them. There is something powerful about just being in the house when our kids are home.

Church. There is a major difference between worshiping in a nearly empty room and a full room. Just the physical presence of others can drastically change an experience.

Community. It matters far more if we vote than how we vote. It matters if we show support for our cities and non-profits.

Physical presence makes a difference.

Knowing the power of presence makes the pastorate very difficult. I'm aware there are many situations and events in which my presence would be an encouragement to others, yet there are too many surgeries, weddings, funerals, trials, and other situations for me to attend each one. Knowing when to be present and when not to be present is one of the most difficult aspects of my job.

In my hometown, a group of citizens is trying to put an end to child abuse. One trend they noticed was how many of the accused were being found not guilty at trial or being charged with lesser crimes. One way they believed this could be changed was by showing prosecutors, judges, and juries that the public wanted these issues taken seriously.

A young teenager had been sexually abused for many years by a family member, but the family didn't believe the boy. At the trial, the defendant had many people there in support of him, but the victim had no support. The trial ended in a deadlocked jury. Hearing about the lack of support, this group got volunteers to go support the victim at the re-trial. This time, the courtroom looked completely opposite. The victim's side was completely full. Not surprisingly, the trial ended in a conviction.

Now, whenever a victim lacks family or friends to support them, this group shows up to give them the support of the community.

Just showing up changes the perception of everyone involved.

We are aware when physical presence influences us in a negative way, but every time we get nervous because of a boss, or slow down because of a police officer, or change our actions because of an authority figure, we should also consider how to use our physical presence to encourage others.

Just showing up will help our kids, spouses, communities, churches, and friends.

I didn't think there was anything wrong with the Facebook post, but I could be wrong.

Clearly, someone thought I was wrong.

I was in Walmart and happened to wander into their book section. The most prominent book displayed in the Christian section was a book allegedly about Biblical prophecy. In my theological opinion it has nothing to do with prophecy or the Bible. It's a get-rich-quick scheme based on scaring people into thinking the world might end tomorrow because of how poorly our political opponents are acting.

So I took a picture and made a slightly humorous comment showing I didn't support the book.

Many people responded to the post—some in support, some attempting humor, and some disagreeing. It was an engaging thread until someone took deep exception to my post. They didn't just disagree with my point, they made deep judgments about my heart. They questioned my role as a pastor; let it be known they would never visit the church I pastor, discouraged others from attending, and said pastors should live to a higher standard.

When I read the critique, two thoughts quickly passed my mind.

First, I wondered if I was guilty. Anytime someone accuses us of something, we should consider their point. Even if we do not like their approach, we should examine our hearts. Maybe the post was out of bounds. Maybe it didn't accomplish what I wanted. Maybe there was a better way to go about it.

Secondly, I wondered why I couldn't see in myself what was so easy to see in others. In other words, how do I fail the way this person failed?

Notice the irony of the comment: a Christian took to Facebook to tell me on Facebook that I should never critique another person on Facebook. As a pastor, they thought I should know better and they were appalled at the condition of my heart which would allow me to be so negative.

My five-year-old self wanted to respond: "So you don't want me to do to others what you just did to me?" But my 36-year-old self restrained my childish response and instead asked the question: "Why can't I see in myself what is so obvious in others."

> "Attacking other people is much easier than reflecting on our own actiions."

It's easy to see fault in other people. They are selfish, condescending, childish, petty, rude, mean, short-sighted, and often wrong. And it's not just that they're all of those things, but they're all of those things in blatant and obvious ways.

Yet common sense tells me I'm not unique. Whatever is so obvious to me about other people is likely very obvious about me to other people. While I may not sin in the exact way, I no doubt sin to the same degree and frequency. So why is it so easy to see in others but so difficult to see in myself?

What are some ways I condemn in others the very thing I'm doing?

It is much more difficult to see our own sin and shortcomings because it takes maturity to do so. A child can easily point at their sibling and tattle. But it takes real maturity to step outside of ourselves, look at our actions objectively, and judge our thoughts or actions as inappropriate. Then it takes tremendous humility to admit fault and confess our imperfections.

Attacking other people is much easier than reflecting on our own actions.

Yet we must do the hard work.

We cannot go through life writing the story that we are good and everyone else is bad. We cannot make it our call to point out the faults of everyone else. We must do the mature work of looking at our own lives.

This doesn't mean we can ignore our responsibility to stand up for truth. Bad actions, ideas, and beliefs do need to be confronted. We can't remain silent. We must walk the fine line of standing on the side of truth with humility and self-confession.

Here are three questions to help us look first at ourselves before others:

1. Whenever we're outraged by others, ask: **What is it within me that causes me to be so outraged by them?** Turn the focus back on your heart and your actions.

2. Whenever we're quick to assume we are holy and someone else is not, ask: **What are some ways I sin in a similar fashion?** Refuse to fall for the delusion that you're morally superior to others.

3. Whenever we are tempted to point out something wrong, ask: **How can I highlight disagreement with an action or idea without attacking the person's heart?**

I'm still open to the thought I shouldn't have posted what I did on Facebook. I don't think I was wrong, but maybe I was. I'm convinced the book is bad and should not be supported, but maybe my attitude was not appropriate.

Yet I wonder less about that one post and more about the posts, comments, and actions that I don't even recognize are wrong. I'm afraid I'm doing to others what I don't like done to me. And I'm doing so without even seeing it.

Your actions and your attitudes. That's it. You control nothing else. You have influence on many other things—your health, friends, family, where you work, etc, but you only control your actions and your attitudes.

And this is good news.

We foolishly believe if we controlled other things life would be better for both us and others. However, we grossly overestimate our ability. Controlling ourselves stretches our capacity so that we have no other time or ability to control anything else.

But we try.

Trying to control others diminishes our ability to control ourselves.

Our ability to control ourselves is indirectly proportional to our attempt to control others. The more we try to control others, the less we can control ourselves. The less we attempt to control others, the more we control ourselves.

If you want to better control yourself, define what you can and cannot control.

The desire to control others often feels noble. We want what's best so we attempt to "help" others make better decisions. The difficulty is that our "help" is often manipulative, coercive, or enabling.

Instead of helping others, we feel responsible for the thoughts, feelings, or actions of others.

Instead of determining our own emotions, we mirror the emotions of others (if my child is sad then I'm sad, if my boss is angry then I'm angry, etc).

Instead of setting our own schedule, our lives are dictated by the perceived needs of others.

Instead of saying "no," we say "yes" even though we don't mean it.

Out of a sense of duty, we do what we don't want to do.

Instead of asking for help, we expect others to just know our needs as we think we know their needs.

Instead of allowing others to experience the negative consequences of their own decisions, we feel the need to rescue them while expecting them to make better decisions next time.

As we attempt to control the lives of others, we slowly lose control of our own actions and attitudes. Our satisfaction in life is determined by what others are doing, thinking, and feeling.

The way to better control ourselves is to recognize we cannot control others.

We can help. We can offer our strengths and abilities. We can model wisdom and offer to do what we can do.

We can care. We can feel a deep sense of compassion and empathy for others.

But we can't control. We can't force people to make wise choices. We can't remove every negative consequence. We can't feel a sense of responsibility for how other people think and feel (even how they think or feel about us).

Two Byproducts of Understanding Control

Whenever we understand what we do and do not control, we experience two natural byproducts.

1. **Less guilt.** A good amount of guilt people face is false guilt. It is a negative emotion based on other people. If we believe we can control others, we will feel guilty when they make bad choices. Even though it isn't our fault, we feel the blame. By understanding that we can't control others, it frees us from the false guilt we often experience.

2. **Empowerment.** Ironically, understanding we don't control as much as we think empowers us because we understand what we do control. No matter the situation, we know we're in complete control of our actions and attitudes. This feeling is empowering. No one can make me feel something or do something. In every circumstance, I control myself.

Whenever I know myself, I'm well aware of my limitations. I know controlling my own actions and attitudes is time-consuming enough. I cannot expend any extra energy attempting to control others.

However, when I lose sight of myself and overestimate my ability and responsibility, I will attempt to control more things than I can. As I do, I will lose control of the one thing I have an opportunity to control—me.

If you want to better control yourself, stop trying to control everyone else.

Notes

11

Conflict

We trust ourselves. If I had to narrow down the most common mistake every person makes, it would be this—we blindly trust what we think occurred without any thought that we might be wrong. We know what we saw. We believe what we heard. The thought never crosses our minds that we only saw the situation from one angle. We never consider that we might have heard wrong.

Humanity has a tremendous capability to process a lot of information in a short period of time. With an unbelievable accuracy, we decipher information and rightly determine what is happening around us. While the accuracy is amazing, we are not as accurate as we think we are. Far more often than we realize, we do not see what happened or we do not hear what was actually said.

On a weekly basis, people give me the privilege of speaking into their lives through both articles and speeches. I consider this a great privilege. Yet on a weekly basis I find myself saying, "Go back and read the article. I didn't write what you claim that I wrote" or "Go back and watch the speech. I didn't say what you claim I said."

With great confidence people confront an idea, never realizing I do not hold the opinion they believe I hold. While it is always fair (and sometimes fun) to debate a topic, it is neither fair nor fun when people assume you believe something you do not.

The most common mistake they make is the most common mistake I make—we trust ourselves too much. We fail to realize how often we get things wrong and this failure gives us a boldness we should rarely have.

The consequences of our confidence is all around us. Most conflict is not birthed from a difference of opinion or wrongdoing. Most conflict is caused by miscommunication. In marriage, at work, or with friends, a majority of the time when we are angry, we are wrongly angry.

Clearly there are times in which anger is justified and useful. Yet most of the time someone is angry with me, it isn't justified. As a leader, I often meet with people who are upset with me. My common start to tense conversations is to smile and say, "Now what am I being accused of?" It's a lighthearted approach with a serious point. I want to hear specifically what the person is upset about and why they are upset. Not every time, but on most occasions, I either haven't done what they think I have done or I did not have the evil intention which they assumed I had. It's almost always a miscommunication.

Of course on occasion, it isn't. In some circumstances I have acted poorly, made a bad choice, or (most often) wrongly acted on my own confidence which I should not have had. Either way, whether their confidence or mine, most conflict I experience is from miscommunication.

This is great news. If most conflict is born of miscommunication that means we can easily solve most conflict. We can't guarantee the same opinion or viewpoint, but we can ease the tension of differences and find common ground.

Here are two steps to prevent most conflicts:

1. **Verify (define the 'what').** Always assume you might have misunderstood, misheard, or didn't see everything that happened. When you are upset with someone, verify what actually took place. Without malice or blame, have a conversation with the person to get their side of the story. Ask fair questions and listen to their answers.

   Ask the other person, from your perspective:

   • What happened?

   • What did you see?

- What did you say?
- What did you hear?

This define the "facts." It clarifies "what" actually happened. Until we clarify the "what," we cannot have a reasonable conversation about any disagreement.

2. **Clarify (define the 'why').** The "what" is important, but it's not the whole story. Just as many conflicts occur over the "why" as the "what." To find common ground, we must also clarify the intentions of those involved. This also occurs best with fair questions, honestly asked.

Ask the other person:

- Why did you choose what you chose?
- Why do you think this situation occurred?
- Why do you think we disagree?
- What did you hope would happen?
- Did you desire the outcome that occurred?

By asking questions of intent, we can determine the heart of the other person. Maybe we agree on the facts, but we have wrongly judged the other person's intentions. As a leader, I often have to tell others, "I might be dead wrong about the decision I made, but even if I'm wrong, we must agree that we have the same intention. We both want what is best, we just disagree on how to make that happen."

Whenever we verify and clarify we are honoring the other person and respecting their humanity. We are giving them room to explain

> "By asking questions of intent, we can determine the heart of the other person. Maybe we agree on the facts, but we have wrongly judged the other person's intentions."

themselves and to be understood. We are providing a climate in which they can admit wrong if they so desire or we can confess that we have incorrectly judged a situation or person. We are being fair.

Whenever we fail to verify or clarify, we are disrespecting everyone else involved. We are wrongly elevating our ability to judge every aspect of the situation. We are devaluing the thoughts, opinions, and experiences of others, determining that they are not worthy of a voice. We are saying our judgment is the only one that matters.

The most common mistake I make is to assume that what I heard is what was said; that what I saw is what actually happened; that what I believe someone intends is actually what they intend. It's a dangerous assumption and one which causes most of the conflict in my life. Thankfully, when I verify and clarify, my judgment is given better information and context.

Don't trust yourself as much as you are tempted to do.

We make two mistakes when it comes to talking about our problems with other people:

Some tell everyone everything.

Some tell no one anything.

Neither is a good option.

While being an open book has noble qualities, few things can destroy our lives as much as failing to have boundaries. Telling everything to everyone can have disastrous consequences.

I see this when an affair is exposed. Often, the hurting spouse will quickly spread the word about what their husband/wife has done. It feels good in the moment. It keeps the spouse from having to put on a front and pretend like everything's okay. It publicly places the blame where it should be placed.

But I've never seen anyone who told everyone everything who didn't later regret it. If the spouse chooses to work on the marriage, having everyone know "their secret" is not helpful. It can sabotage the marriage recovery as each gives their two cents' worth about what the couple should do.

Conversely, I know people who never tell anyone anything. On the surface this appears as a great strength. Yet the appearance of stoicism is not strength. It's weakness cloaked in power. It's dangerous.

No one was created to navigate this world on their own. No matter the pain and sorrow of past relationships, everyone should risk inviting someone into their lives and sharing their problems with them.

This raises a key question: Whom should I tell of my struggles?

When it comes to private issues, I would recommend only telling your problems to two types of people:

Only tell someone who can help. This is the most important rule when in the midst of a difficult situation. It provides a guardrail to keep you from telling too many people. Only tell those who can help you deal with the issue. When I meet with couples who are dealing with an affair, I advise them—tell one friend, one pastor, and one counselor. The friend can help you with the details of life, the pastor can assist you spiritually, and the counselor can help your marriage. Don't tell anyone else unless it's absolutely necessary. While it may feel necessary to tell every friend and family member, it will not be helpful. Remember, you can always decide later to tell someone else, but once you tell someone, you cannot take it back.

Think twice before you tell once.

Only tell someone if it can help. After you've navigated a tough time, there's a second group you can tell. If hearing your story can help someone else, tell them. Stories are powerful and we can often leverage them to assist others. Generally, telling our story in the midst of the struggle is not helpful, but once we get a step or two down the road, we can use our stories to assist others. This takes courage, transparency, and vulnerability, but it's often worth it.

We all deal with problems. Some situations tempt us to tell everyone. Other situations tempt us to tell no one. Rarely is either of those options appropriate. By only telling someone who can help and someone who it can help, we maintain our privacy while also joining others in healthy community.

There is more going on than what you see.

One of the most amazing places the pastorate takes me is the NICU. It can be the saddest place in my life, but most often it's the most hopeful place. Most of the babies I see in the NICU grow up to have wonderful lives.

It always strikes me as I'm standing in the NICU that healing is taking place. It doesn't look like healing. It looks as though nothing is happening, but as the babies bask under the warming lamps, their bodies are at work closing holes in lungs, clearing fluid, maturing under-developed organs, and growing.

Healing is often an unseen process.

Over the weekend I went to the NICU to visit twins. As we walked back and forth between the two incubators, the parents recounted the words of the doctor that the twins can sense each other. Even though they're separated by several feet, the doctor assumes they know the other is near. It's his desire to get them together as quickly as possible.

He told the parents he rarely sends one twin home while the other remains in the hospital because he believes it threatens the health of the stronger twin. In empathy for its sibling, the twin sent home is often sent back to the hospital because of declining health.

As I stood and looked at these two babies sleeping a few feet apart, it looked to my untrained eye like very little was happening. But there was far more going on than I could see.

It's true not just for newborns, it's true for us all.

There is always more going on than what we see.

It's true on a personal level. We like to believe we've dealt with the issues from our past and that we're independent agents making decisions with complete free will. However, the truth is, history, experiences, and influences are always expressing themselves through the decisions we make and how we feel. A bad experience, which has never been processed, is certainly expressing itself in a negative way—whether it be through overeating, anxiety, an unwillingness to build close friendships, or an inability to be still and quiet.

It's true on a community level. As we interact with others, we make snap judgments based on what we see, but we rarely see the whole picture. There's always more going on that causes the employee to be late, the co-worker to be frustrated, the teacher to be disheveled, or the nurse to be hurried. While we see the complexity within our own lives, we often assume simplicity in the lives of others. We judge others as uncaring, inept, or evil, never realizing they're hurting, confused, and just trying to cope with life.

It's true on a spiritual level. Faith says there's more to life than meets the eye. What's interesting is with every scientific development, research is verifying that we see but a small part of a much larger picture. As one twin can influence his sibling, even though they're physically separated, so too, what we consider merely physical realities have spiritual connotations and meanings. There is a God we cannot see. There are eternal ramifications to temporal decisions. This world is all we see, but it's not all there is.

> The great danger is that we'll trust our eyes just to the extent that we won't believe anything we can't see. We'll fail to consider other possibilities, and in so doing we'll believe in far less than there actually is.

The choice between faith and a lack of faith is often the difference between believing we see everything or only a few things. As a person of faith, I believe I see only a part of the complete complexity of what is.

There is more going on than what you see.

Every Sunday I speak on two different occasions for around 40 minutes. Every week I write five posts of about 750 words each. Every day I lead a non-profit organization made up of hundreds of volunteers.

Needless to say, there are occasions when people disagree with me.

I've noticed something about these disagreements. Some are effective critiques that cause me to evaluate my own opinion and strengthen my relationship with that person, even if we don't end up with the same ideas. Others are damaging events that cause me to hold tighter to my opinions and distance myself from the person raising the issue.

There is only one difference between the two.

People who are effective at offering useful critiques refuse to make an issue personal.

The number one rule of disagreement is do not make it personal.

It sounds like an obvious rule, but it's one that's difficult to follow.

No matter our background or experience, our tendency is to state our position and then to do everything in our power to prove our point—to win the argument.

The desire to defeat the other person rather than understand them makes it tempting to allow our opinion to define that person. Instead of discussing an issue, we question their mind, heart, and soul. Surely if they don't think like what we think, something must be wrong with them.

Of course, this viewpoint is wrong on two levels:

1. **We always assume there's a clear right or wrong about a specific issue.** We assume this even though issues are rarely black and white. Even when most of the world agrees on an

issue, like our need to stop terrorism, no one is sure how to do so and many plans are offered as possible solutions. While a few issues are clearly right or wrong, many are not.

2. **We always assume we're right.** We assume this even though every aspect of our lives reveals we're often wrong. It's sadly humorous when a person who can't balance his own family budget is frustrated because politicians struggle with the complexities of international finance.

Issues are rarely black and white and even when they are, we're rarely right.

We cannot deny disagreements. We can't hide from them or ignore them. We must be able to openly communicate with others, including freely expressing disagreeing viewpoints.

But there is one basic rule nearly every person violates when voicing dissent. The number one rule of disagreement is do not make it personal.

It's a common tendency when voicing dissent to take a disagreement in idea or belief and make it into a discussion of which person is better. This habit has disastrous consequences. It causes:

- marriages to end
- communities to languish
- churches to split
- friendships to fracture
- businesses to die

Our inability to discuss the actual issue and our necessity to win an argument is childish, dishonest, and deeply painful to ourselves and others.

Ironically, the less certain we are about our opinion, the more likely we are to be vicious to those we disagree with.

In our attempt to win arguments, we often raise an issue, but then deflect from the actual disagreement and pile on other issues, in hopes of showing how wrong the other person is. And if we can't pile on other issues, we attack the person's character or heart.

Consider:

- Is the president wrong or is he evil?
- Did the referee miss a call or did he try to steal the game?
- Does the other person have a different perspective than you or are they stupid?

Why can't we just disagree? Why do we have to make the issue personal? Why do we have to question a person's character, intent, patriotism, and faith just because we see an issue differently?

We don't and we shouldn't.

Knowing the human temptation to make disagreements personal, we should approach them in a different way:

We should expect them more often. The more aware we are of our own imperfections, the more we should expect others to disagree with our thoughts and viewpoints. We all have a variety of opinions, so disagreements will arise. If you often have disagreements with the people you love the most (your family), why should it surprise you when other people disagree with your opinion or idea?

We should approach them more carefully. Because of our tendency to make issues personal, we should be cognizant of that temptation when we approach a confrontation and careful about the words we choose.

We should conclude them more humbly. Even if we conclude a disagreement while still disagreeing, we should end the discussion in a humble way. I could be wrong, you could be wrong, we both could be right, we both could be wrong, etc. And even if you are wrong on this issue, I know I'm wrong on other issues, so I should never allow your being wrong about one issue to define my whole perception of who you are as a person.

When we do these three things, we will be more likely to stay on topic and refuse the temptation of making things personal.

Feel free to disagree, just don't question my intelligence, compassion, or faith as you do so.

"Why can't we just disagree? Why do we have to make the issue personal? Why do we have to question a person's character, intent, patriotism, and faith just because we see an issue differently?

We don't and we shouldn't."

Some people are addicted to drama. It's a drug that triggers a part of their brains causing them to crave the activity.

They claim they hate drama, even as they call you, post on Facebook, and tell the latest tale to anyone willing to listen.

They're like meth addicts who claim to hate the stuff even as their teeth fall out, their skin ages, and they no longer resemble their driver's license photo.

Early in my ministry, I was helping a woman who was living in a chaotic situation. She had made some bad choices and the consequences were difficult. She had surrounded herself with bad people and was suffering because of it. But over time, we worked through some things and the drama of her life settled down.

Two months later, she was back in my office. She had repeated the same choices as before. Despite all the work to escape the drama, she had run right back to it.

We began the process over. After weeks of hard work and navigating several tough issues, she was free. But of course, a few months later she called again.

I finally realized, it didn't matter how many times I helped this woman, she would always repeat the decisions to get back into a chaotic situation.

It was the only life she knew. Like a person in bankruptcy who wins the lottery only to lose it all again, this woman didn't know how to live a life of peace.

If given the choice of peace or drama, she would choose drama, while claiming she hated it.

Like many people, she was addicted. She couldn't help herself. Without serious intervention, help, and a great deal of work, she would forever seek, find, or create drama.

If drama often finds you, it might be worth asking: Why?

Of course, drama is part of life. Every office, social group, family, or any gathering of people will have episodes of drama—crises will arise, conflict will occur, tension will build. Drama in this life is guaranteed.

But continual drama is not a natural consequence of life. A normal flow of peaceful times and chaotic times should be expected. Rare seasons of frequent turmoil are normal. But at some point, an overwhelming amount of drama could be a signal, not that drama is finding us, but that we're finding it.

Here are a few common characteristics of Drama Addicts:

1. **An uncanny ability to see conflict even when it doesn't exist.** Generally speaking, you will find what you're looking for. Look for peace and you'll find it. Look for conflict and you'll find it. Drama addicts are constantly looking for their drug, and so, they often find it.

2. **An inability to stay out of conflict even when it isn't their business.** Healthy people know if a conflict is their business or not. A drama addict sees every conflict as something they have to involve themselves in and take sides. They are unable to realize that most conflict is not our business and does not require our involvement. The first question anyone should ask when facing a situation is: "Is this my responsibility?" Most often the answer is "no."

3. **A belief that a state of drama, and not a state of peace, should be the norm.** Most drama addicts believe if they're experiencing peace, something must be wrong. They're surprised by it. They're uncomfortable with it. This uneasiness is what causes them to seek out problems or even create them. They don't know how to handle an absence of drama.

The problem with being addicted to drama is the same problem as any other addiction. It doesn't satisfy. It is exhausting. It's a horrible way to live.

Life doesn't have to be this way.

There are other options.

You can live a life:

- with a small amount of drama that doesn't overwhelm you
- with a deep satisfaction of life and your relationships
- with an ability to help others without taking on their problems
- with an ability to feel empathy for others without feeling overwhelmed
- with proper boundaries

All this is possible. But to live this way will require you to admit you have a problem, understand you are powerless over it, and seek assistance in living a radically different life.

Everyone faces drama. Seasons come and seasons go. If you find yourself facing an unusual amount of drama on a regular basis, it might be time to get help.

Offensive people are all around. They work in the cubicle next to us. They dominate our Facebook news feed. They coach our child's rival t-ball team.

Every day we're forced to interact with people who knowingly or unknowingly are offensive.

Here's a comprehensive plan to deal with offensive people:

Step 1--Choose not to be offended.

That's it. Choose not to be offended.

One of the greatest misconceptions we have about other people is the belief that they have the power to offend us. They don't.

Other people do not offend us, we choose to get offended.

Many times we have a right to be offended, but it's our choice nonetheless. And we make that choice far too often.

Most of what offends us, shouldn't. Much of what makes our blood boil, what divides relationships, and what irritates us, shouldn't. What should be minor situations that are overlooked, often become the most memorable aspect of our day.

Instead of choosing to be offended, we can have empathy, understanding, and compassion. Just as we appreciate others being understanding with our failed attempts at communication, we can be understanding with theirs.

Here are several ways to prevent being offended:

Give the benefit of the doubt. Whenever someone says something offensive, consider scenarios in which their words or actions aren't offensive. Most people don't willfully attempt to be offensive. Their words might come across in a way they didn't intend. We should try to understand their intent. Assume they weren't trying to offend.

Understand we all make mistakes. Even if we have a right to be offended, remembering a time when we were offensive should give us compassion. Seeing the words or actions of another as a mistake prevents us from taking great offense.

See their offense as their problem. When a person is repetitively offensive, we should see their behavior as their problem instead of taking it personally. We can remind ourselves their behavior has nothing to do with us. Whether we're present or not, the person would be offensive. They either have the inability to change or have chosen not to. Either way, the problem is theirs and has nothing to do with us.

Define your own emotions. No matter the situation, make sure your emotions are defined by you and not by others. You choose how you feel. Don't give the authority over your emotions to another person. Make your own choices.

Many people are looking to be offended. They seek out offense and proudly announce how they've been victimized. But it doesn't have to be this way. The easiest way to deal with offensive people is to choose not to be offended so easily.

The other person probably didn't mean to be offensive. Even if they did, how many times have we been offensive? Even if they're much more offensive than we've ever been, it's their problem. And no matter what their problem is, I'm in charge of my own emotions and life.

Make people work hard if they want to offend you.

Try it today. Every time you're tempted to be offended, choose not to be and see what happens.

"The easiest way to deal with offensive people is to choose not to be offended so easily."

Notes

12

Grief

What is one universal topic that influences the largest number of people, but is widely unknown or unrecognized?

Grief.

One of the great guarantees of life is that we will all lose. Life cannot be lived without loss.

We're well aware of grief in the traumatic losses of life.

Nothing can compare to the loss of a child.

Nothing can prepare us for the death of a parent.

Unless you've gone through it, you can't know the fear of a terminal diagnosis.

We're aware of grief in these situations, but even though we're all guaranteed extreme loss, most of us are still gravely unaware of what that grief entails.

Beyond our ignorance of the grief process, we're also unaware of the presence of grief in our daily lives.

Every day we experience small losses. They don't compare to the traumatic losses of life, but they do create subtle symptoms of grief that influence our mood, thinking, and actions.

Losing is a part of life, and every loss hurts to some degree.

- parents aging
- a child diagnosed
- being laid off
- dreams unrealized
- relationships ending

Life is full of losses both large and small. We are foolish if we think the pain of life doesn't have a regular impact on us.

It is such a part of life that even good events can create symptoms of grief. Many parents experience aspects of grief when their child enters kindergarten. While they're excited for the child's growth, they're grieving the end of the preschool years.

While every grief is unique, there are basic qualities grief shares. Understanding its effects can help us cope, prevent us from making unwise decisions, and provide empathy to ourselves and others.

It's a regular occurrence. I'm visiting a patient in the hospital and a family member is telling me about a test that was ordered but not performed, a lab that was lost, a doctor who never showed up, the meal that was late, etc. As I'm listening, a nurse will walk in and a family member will snap at her. The snap has little to do with the test, lab, doctor, or meal. It rarely has anything to do with the specific nurse. It's nearly always a by product of grief.

The family member snaps because they're tired, frustrated, and hurting. They snap at the nurse because they can.

Anger is a classic aspect of grief. Yet anger is often misplaced. One event or situation causes us to have anger, but we express the anger toward something else. How many times have you spoken harshly to your spouse or child after a long day? You are mad about work, but you express it toward your family.

That's what most often happens in a hospital. The family is grieving for their loved one while also enduring the exhaustion of the hospital stay, but without realizing the presence of grief, they take it out on a nurse who is only trying to do her job.

How else does grief express itself? It's easy for me to spot it in someone else's life while in a hospital room, but how does it express itself in my life? In what ways am I being impatient with people because I'm grieving? How is the presence of grief influencing my thinking or actions in ways that I'm not even aware?

Elisabeth Kubler-Ross famously describes grief in five stages: denial, anger, bargaining, depression, and acceptance. These stages are not like steps on a path that a person walks in linear fashion; instead, they are phases a person continually weaves in and out of.

Most of us live in a continual state of denial, unaware that the pains of life are taking a toll on us emotionally, physically,

> "Whenever we live in denial (or ignorance) of grief, we empower the grief to have a greater negative influence on our lives."

psychologically, and spiritually. We deny the presence of the hurt, or assume the pain will quickly pass when things return to the way they once were. We downplay hurts because they don't compare to the pains of others.

While it is true that getting a demotion doesn't compare to losing a loved one, we cannot deny the grief that comes from a career set-back.

Whenever we live in denial (or ignorance) of grief, we empower the grief to have a greater negative influence on our lives.

Understanding the process of grief cannot save us from it, but it can minimize its effects on our lives.

Knowing grief results in anger can prevent us from snapping at an innocent person, or give us tremendous grace when we're the object of another person's anger.

Realizing the weariness loss creates can cause us to use even greater care when making decisions during times of grief.

Being aware of our temptation toward denial can force us to take the pains of life more seriously.

Many smart people have no idea the influence grief has. Grief can make smart people do dumb things. Grief unchecked is the root cause of many divorces, bankruptcies, addictions, and a plethora of other bad consequences.

The good news is that smart people have the ability to learn new things. By researching the process of grief and reflecting on the pains of one's own life, a person can learn to properly cope, and also be a great ally to others.

I've probably used the phrase ten times in the last week. Through a variety of situations—death, divorce, disappointment—I've reminded the person I'm talking to that the nature of grief is "ever changing."

One of the great deceptions we have about grief is that we have dealt with it. It's what the courageous among us do; we confront the pains of life as they come our way. Some choose a different path. They pretend everything is okay. They're afraid to face the sorrow, so they never deal with it.

But the courageous do. They confront every pain and try to understand it in the context of moving forward. They deal with it.

Yet dealing with our grief can lead to the false assumption that we've dealt with it, as though it's done. We think we've dealt with our grief like we've dealt a stack of cards. It's viewed as a past event.

Most of life's sorrows are not things that can be dealt with one time. We don't get the privilege of one cry, or one month of sadness, or one difficult season to put the loss of a parent, the heartache of a broken relationship, or the diagnosis of a child, behind us.

The deep sorrows of life are not feelings we can get over by dealing with them; they are wounds that forever live with us and are morphing with each passing month.

It's an ever-changing grief.

Having a child with special needs includes grief. Life is not exactly how I want it to be for her and, in turn, it's not exactly how I want it for us. The difference between what is and what should be results in grief. It was true when the diagnosis came and it's true nearly a decade later. But it is always changing:

It was a raw wound the night of the diagnosis.

It grew into a numb confusion for the first few years.

It was a hint of hidden sadness amidst the joys of the toddler years.

It's a quiet stoicism in the elementary years.

But it's all grief.

We dealt with it at birth, continued to deal with it that first year, and still have regular conversations about it now. We have dealt with, and will continue to deal with it, for the rest of our lives.

So it is with grief. It's always there and it's always changing.

No matter how much you grieved the loss of your parent at a young age, you will have to re-grieve their absence with every major milestone. No matter how prepared you are for the death of a loved one, you cannot be fully prepared for the moment they breathe their last, or when you walk into the funeral, or for the first anniversary of their death.

No matter how much you've dealt with the miscarriage or inability to get pregnant, just the right word or song can bring a flood of new emotions to the surface.

Many are confused by the process. They take the presence of grief as a sign they've done something wrong, or as proof they didn't deal with the loss effectively in the months and years after it happened. But the new emotions are not a sign of past failure. It is the basic nature of the grieving process. It never truly ends.

The deepest sorrows will be carried with you the rest of your life. You deal with them, but you have never fully dealt with them.

When we understand the true nature of grief, we're more patient with ourselves, kinder to others, and have a better grasp of what we're feeling, thinking, and doing.

We're able to prepare for difficult times and are not caught off guard when our emotions get the best of us.

Grief is a process, but it's not a simple four-stage process where you travel through each stage and come out healed on the other side. It's a lifetime process you swing in and out of, filled with different emotions based on the current circumstances of your life.

I have grieved over my daughter's diagnosis. I am grieving her diagnosis. And a day will come when I will have to grieve aspects of her diagnosis I haven't even considered yet.

I'm regularly asked, "What's it like having a child with special needs?" I give many answers, but eventually I include, "It's an ever-changing grief." As it is with parenting a child with special needs, so it is with every sorrow of life.

Life will not go as you expect. It will be full of heartbreak and disappointments. Even the most charmed lives will have moments of great sorrow.

One of the most important life skills is being able to navigate disappointments without allowing them to destroy us.

Here's a simple, effective, three-step guide which provides a M.A.P. for navigating life's disappointments:

1. **Mourn what was lost.** Admit it. Name it. Weep over it.

   We live in a day when we no longer know how to mourn. Our society has hidden mourning from view, and the result is that no one knows how to do it anymore. Failing to mourn doesn't make the situation better. It buries feelings that end up expressing themselves in other ways.

   Rather than living in denial, we need to intentionally mourn every heartbreak. Some things can be mourned in minutes, while others won't be overcome in a lifetime. Either way, we need to mourn.

   Mourn the small things, even if your loss doesn't compare to the loss of others. If we were only allowed to mourn if our loss was greater than others, then only one person in the world would be able to mourn at a time.

   Mourn the big things by breaking them into small things. Many live in denial and don't even know it because they're mourning in general and not in the specifics. The loss of a child is more than one loss. It's the loss of a thousand things. By mourning each specific loss as it comes to mind, we're processing the depth of the tragedy. We should cry every tear that needs to be cried.

2. **Appreciate what you have.** Admit it. Name it. Rejoice over it.

   Families who continue to express gratitude in the midst of

difficult situations navigate life better. They don't feel loss less, but they are aware of the positives around them. Those who only focus on the negative feel the same amount of loss, but experience none of the positives. This multiplies the negative.

If we aren't intentional, one disappointment can color how we look at every aspect of life. Nearly every tragic situation is also seasoned with grace—medical professionals who show extraordinary care and compassion for a dying loved one, friends who show deep concern in meaningful ways during your grief, the presence of a loving family being and doing everything a good family is supposed to.

Appreciating the presence of good during a difficult time keeps an individual from despair. Life can hurt deeply, but rarely does that hurt define everything about life. Good is often intermingled within our greatest sorrows.

3. **Prepare for what's ahead.** See it. Anticipate it. Be energized by it.

   Every positive has negatives and every negative has positives. No matter the cause of a disappointment, it results in us being somewhere we never wanted to be. While the new road is not of our choosing, it can be meaningful. And it can be satisfying in ways we could have never expected.

   Choosing to walk this new path with excitement and anticipation is one of the keys to not allowing one disappointment to ruin our life. Feel the sorrow but continue to live.

Everyone experiences disappointments. Some we can avoid, but many we cannot. Knowing how to navigate the disappointments is one of the greatest skills we can learn. The process is not complex, but the courage to walk each step is a tremendous challenge.

I've buried a lot of people who had a friend tell them, "I know you'll be fine."

They weren't fine. They died. And their friends were liars.

They didn't mean to be liars. They didn't want to be liars, but they were.

It goes like this.

A friend gets diagnosed with cancer and someone says, "I know you'll be fine."

There's only one problem. They don't know.

You don't know; I don't know; they don't know; no one knows.

A man once came to my office to plan his funeral. He came alone. When I asked where his family was, he said, "They all say I'm going to be fine. But I'm not going to be fine; I'm going to die." He was right.

In his family's stubbornness, they missed some great conversations about life, death, and the unknown. And tragically, their loved one suffered alone.

There are two reasons we tell people, "I know you will be fine":

1. **We can't handle the unknown.** The phrase—"I know you'll be fine"—is actually a phrase of denial. We're pretending everything is okay, when in reality everything is not okay. At a minimum, there's a threat that something might be wrong. Instead of living in the mystery of the unknown, we choose to live in denial. While denial can be useful at times, it's rarely helpful to others. When we live in denial, what we actually end up denying are the experiences of others. We say, "I know you'll be fine," and what they hear is, "I don't want to talk about this," or, "You shouldn't be worried about this." We're denying their experiences for the sake of our comfort.

2. **We don't want to take the time to talk about it.** We sometimes use the phrase because we don't want to expend the energy or effort to be involved.

"I know you'll be fine, so there is no need for us to talk about it."

"I know you'll be fine, so let's not take the time to discuss your feelings."

"I know you'll be fine, so let's talk about me."

Others are worried, but we reassure them, "I know you'll be fine." In reality, we're reassuring ourselves that we don't have to be involved in the situation.

> The real problem with the phrase is that some believe it's the answer of faith.

They say, "I know you'll be fine because by His stripes we are healed," all the while forgetting that the famous passage from Isaiah has very little to do with whether or not you have cancer.

They say, "I know you'll be fine because God never desires His children to suffer," all the while ignoring the suffering of nearly every follower of Jesus found in Bible.

They say, "I know you'll be fine because God loves you," implying that if things don't go well maybe God's love is a little less.

This phrase of denial has become a token phrase of pseudo-spirituality and it's time for us to stop using it.

You might be fine, but you might not. The fact is that none of us know. So I can't say, "I know you'll be fine."

So, what can we say when a test is coming up, or a diagnosis comes, or someone's facing a time of uncertainty?

- "I'm sorry."
- "I love you."
- "What's your greatest fear?"
- "How can I pray for you?"
- "What does that feel like?"
- "I don't know what to say."
- "What's a good thing to say to someone in your situation?"

All these statements are more truthful, heartfelt, and meaningful than saying, "I know you'll be fine." We might hope it, but we don't know it. And saying it never leads to the outcome we desire.

A simple piece of advice—never buy a house on your way home from the funeral.

It's a rather amazing concept: We can take two substances, which by themselves are harmless, but have an explosive effect when combined.

- chlorine and ammonia
- gasoline and a match
- alcohol and Mel Gibson

By themselves, they are stable, but put together, they are volatile.

I once had a meeting with an attorney. He walked in a few minutes late, gave me one look, and said, "Two dead, rich parents and two ungrateful adult children." He didn't need to say any more.

There is not a more explosive combination than money and grief. It's the cause of many a family fight at the funeral. It's the reason the average widow blows through her spouse's life insurance in just months. It's the reason the shopoholic can't control her spending.

Grief creates sorrow money can temporarily soothe. There's never a worse time to spend than while in grief. Our vision is blurred. Our wounds are exposed. Our ability to think is compromised. If ever we should not be making decisions, it's while we're grieving. Yet it is at this very time we're most likely to spend.

Grief is not just experienced at the funeral home. We all experience grief.

- Life doesn't turn out the way we wish.
- A diagnosis is given.
- A child grows up.
- A promotion is delayed.
- A season in life is over.

Grief can come in many formats. When it happens, we must be careful.

Here are several suggestions regarding how to spend money in times of grief:

Slow down. Grief speeds up our decision making. To make a wise choice, we must slow down. Never buy anything on impulse when you're grieving.

Seek advice. Grief limits our ability to see beyond ourselves. Advisors have the skills to assist us in times of trouble.

Heal, then spend. Instead of trying to cope with grief by spending, work with someone to explore your grief, in hopes of finding healing. If you're experiencing a cycle of debt, it could be that underlying grief is making it difficult for you to get a handle on your finances.

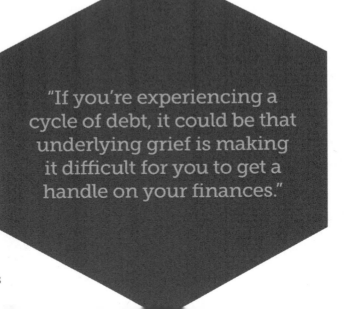

"If you're experiencing a cycle of debt, it could be that underlying grief is making it difficult for you to get a handle on your finances."

What do you do on your worst day?

When your wife dies?

When your child is arrested?

When your marriage ends?

When your trust is broken?

When life as you know it is no more?

On a weekly basis, I'm with people as their lives are dramatically changed.

- The new grandmother entering her favorite chapter of life is suddenly gone.
- The rock of a man is diagnosed and withers to a shadow of his former self.
- The perfect child makes a life-altering decision.
- A day that begins with a normal drive to work, ends with an emergency helicopter ride to a trauma unit.
- What is supposed to be a normal week is blown up by an accusation, an arrest, and a family's name brought to shame.

The examples are endless.

But what should you do?

Only one thing comes to mind.

March Madness has one motto: Survive and Advance.

As college basketball teams pursue their dreams of a National Championship, it doesn't matter how well they play, by how much they win, or if they meet expectations. The only thing that matters is if they find a way to win the game. As long as they stay alive, they have a chance to accomplish their dreams. The motto of every NCAA basketball team is "survive and advance."

It should be the same motto we use whenever we face an overwhelming situation.

When it comes to grief, many have high expectations. They think they must:

- learn a great lesson
- be the model of perfection
- show strength for their family
- be a testimony to others
- avoid any outward displays of sorrow

Many of these attributes are noble. If a great sorrow came into my life, I would love to be the perfect example of how to handle tragedy with bold faith and deep trust.

But what if I don't?

What if I didn't learn a great lesson?

What if I struggled with doubt and uncertainty?

What if I wasn't able to "be strong" for my family, or be an example for others?

What if I fell apart? Doubted everything? And wasn't sure what tomorrow would hold?

It wouldn't greatly matter.

There are moments when we should learn lessons. We should regularly seek to be an example to others and give a testimony to the faith we hold. Most of the time, we should serve others and assist them. All of these are good goals to pursue in most situations.

However, there are moments when we can forget all these goals. At times, the sorrow is so overwhelming that we can rightly set a lower bar for success.

When grief is overwhelming, have one goal: survive and advance.

Forget the great lesson.

Don't worry about what others think.

Know there will be another day to serve others.
Simply survive and advance.

Survive:
- keep breathing
- try to sleep
- eat
- do whatever is minimally necessary to live

Advance:
- work the steps
- seek direction from others
- accept help
- get counseling
- cry every tear necessary
- confront your emotions

Survive and advance doesn't sound like the most noble of pursuits, but it is the most useful advice possible.

Difficult times can bring opportunities to learn great lessons and teach great things. But nothing will be learned or taught, no example will be given or testimony presented, if we do not endure the dark days.

There are times when you can decide to learn later. Speak later. Work later. And be an example later.

When times are at their worst, just try to survive today. All those other things can wait until tomorrow.

You need to feel sad.

Not all the time.

Not even most of the time.

But some times, more often than you desire, you need to feel sorrow.

And in some seasons of life, your sorrow may be long-lasting.

We live in a diagnosis culture. Every ailment, every illness, every set of symptoms awaits a proper diagnosis. It's a great aspect of our times. I often tell patients before surgery, "Today is the best day to ever have what you have. The only possible better day would be tomorrow."

Technology and science have expanded the capabilities of skilled professionals, empowering them to solve many issues, from life-threatening illnesses to common annoyances.

Yet this culture has a downside.

The prevailing expectation is that every hurt, sorrow, sadness, and grief should be diagnosed and cured. By popping a pill, doing an exercise, or having a session, the expectation is that we can quickly eradicate our sadness.

We can't.

And we shouldn't try.

Without question, some sorrow can, and should, be eliminated.

Many carry around the baggage from past experiences, hurts, or mistakes, and the sadness lingers for years. Their denial, which creates an unwillingness to confront the past issues, causes a single event to define whole decades of their lives.

Others experience chemical or biological changes, which create anxiety or depression. Medication can often help.

But not every tear needs a diagnosis. Not every pain should be cured.

Sadness, sorrow, and grief are important parts of life. While we should never force negative emotions, we should embrace them as a vital element of processing our world.

At times, we should be sad.

Yet in today's Dr. Phil and pop-a-pill culture, we assume sadness is a sign that something's wrong. Often, however, it's a sign that something is right.

Sorrow can be for our benefit. It can call us out of denial and into reality. Not everything will go our way. We will experience loss. We will grieve. Heartache and dashed dreams are unavoidable.

Whenever we label every sadness as a diagnosable condition, we're implying two things:

1. Sadness isn't justified unless it can be explained (and specifically diagnosed).

2. Every sadness is in need of a cure.

We diagnose every tear. A diagnosis gives justification for our sorrow. Without the justification, we feel our grief is invalid. No wonder we feel this way when our society is so uncomfortable with any expression of sorrow. Before you can shed a tear, someone will hand you a Kleenex. It looks like compassion, but it's actually a quick announcement that tears are not welcome. We expect people to grieve in private, cry in a closet, and after they've regained their composure, they're welcomed back to the real world.

In a world where everyone is expected to answer, "I'm good," when asked, "How are you doing?" is it any wonder we feel the need to justify our sadness?

The justification is also about our greater desire for a cure. If we can diagnose it, we can solve it.

Sorrow and grief are the emotional equivalent of a childhood fever. Many pediatricians believe a fever is a useful mechanism. It can be a sign the body is fighting a cold. But try telling that to a concerned parent. Most parents just want the fever to be gone.

The same is true with sorrow. We just want it gone, even if the argument can be made that it's useful. We want to diagnose our sadness so we can figure out the proper prescription. People look to me for the perfect prayer, while others look to doctors for the right pill, or to the psychologist for the right session. Whatever it takes, fix the sorrow so we can be happy again.

But this is a dangerous way to look at sadness. Rather than diagnosing every tear, it might be better to cry every tear. To grieve the great sorrows of life could be one of the most productive and healthy processes we can endure. Rather than trying to figure everything out, or diagnosing everything, just be sad. Recognize it, and admit it. Understand you won't feel this way forever, and process through the sorrow.

You might not be able to do it alone. You might need help, either from a friend, a pastor, or a professional. But the normal sorrows of life are just that. They are normal. The quicker we become comfortable with grief and sadness, the kinder we'll be to ourselves and others, whenever we face the sorrows of life.

Not every tear needs a diagnosis.

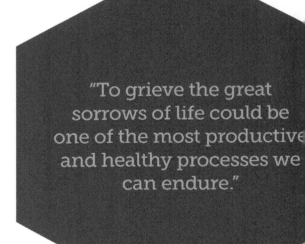

"To grieve the great sorrows of life could be one of the most productive and healthy processes we can endure."

A few years ago we experienced extreme summer drought. Every tree suffered, but as the summer gave way to the fall it was obvious that eight trees in my backyard were dead. I needed to remove them, but I waited too late. As fall gave way to winter, there was no way for me to determine which trees were dormant and which were dead.

Imagine if this was your first experience with seasons. As summer turned to fall you would be amazed at the beauty and colors, but as winter took hold, you would be in shock. You would assume everything was dead. No matter how much others told you not to worry, it would be impossible to imagine trees, flowers, or grasses coming back to life. In your mind they are dead and dead things do not come back to life.

Of course, everyone who has experienced the seasons knows that trees, flowers, and grasses aren't dead in the winter; they are simply dormant. Allow the weather to warm up and everything will begin to bloom and green again.

There is a difference between dormant and dead. Just like the trees in my backyard during the middle of winter, the two look alike. Yet time reveals what is dead and what is dormant.

On a regular basis I deal with people who believe something is dead—their marriage, career, faith, life.

The feelings are gone. The signs of life have vanished. All hope is lost.

They think it is dead, but I wonder if it's dormant.

> I wonder if:
>
> **with a little attention and heat, their marriage can bloom back to life.**
>
> **with a little effort and intention, their career can bounce back.**
>
> **with prayer and study, their relationship with God can grow again.**

One of the most frustrating aspects of being a pastor is dealing with people who are convinced something is dead, when I know it's not. Having never been through an experience like what they're going through, they can't imagine feelings for their spouse coming back or a relationship with God being reborn or life being any different than what it is. Because they haven't seen what can happen, they look at something that's dormant and assume it's dead.

I know better. I've seen people change, marriages come alive, addictions cease, and prodigals return.

Most of the time when something looks dead, it's only dormant. However, if we treat it as though it's dead, it will become a self-fulfilling prophecy.

Treat your marriage/career/life as dead and they will die. Treat them as dormant—give them attention, do the work, get help—and they will likely come back to life.

Take a look at the trees. They look dead. It takes a great deal of faith to believe they will ever bloom again, but of course they will. Look at your life. Whatever looks dead is probably only dormant. Have faith, do the work, and watch it bloom again.

Conclusion

Find the Privilege

You have given me a privilege.

By reading this book, you have given me entry into your life. It might just be for a few hours, but you have kindly granted me the privilege of speaking to you.

Whenever I lose sight of the privilege, writing can become tedious. Coming up with an idea, pounding out the words, and then revising until I get it right, can feel like a job.

But when I remember the privilege, my whole approach is different. Each element of the process is a step toward this great gift people have given me.

As it is in writing, so it is in life. As long as we remember the privilege we've been given, the process will be an honor, a life-breathing gift. But the moment we lose sight of the privilege, everything becomes burdensome.

I often begin wedding ceremonies with an explanation of the giving of the bride. While giving away the bride comes from a less-than-honorable tradition when women were viewed as property, the act can serve as great symbolism for the bride and groom. I instruct the groom to look at the father and consider what the father is doing. He's giving away one of his most valuable treasures. He has agreed to give the bride to the groom. For as long as the bride and groom view each other as a gift they've been given, they will do the work necessary for the marriage to thrive. But the moment they view one another as an entitlement, the marriage will be in trouble.

Life is full of privilege. People grant us access into their lives that we don't deserve. We are given time, attention, and a variety of other gifts that are easily overlooked.

Whenever we lose sight of the privilege, we lose heart for the person. We focus on the task instead of the person. Life becomes work rather than a gift.

Beyond marriage, consider the privilege in:

Leadership. Leading a group is a great gift. They trust you enough to listen and follow. They allow you to set the course. They submit themselves to your direction.

Parenting. Who deserves to be a parent? While parenting is exhausting, it's also one of life's greatest privileges. As a pastor, I'm well aware of many people who would do anything to have a baby. While some assume getting pregnant and giving birth is easy, I know what a great gift it is. Clearly, a parent can't see the privilege in every moment, but we should stop and thank God for allowing us to be parents.

Work. Most people don't like their jobs, yet having a job is a privilege. This doesn't mean you have to keep the job you have, or you can't look for another one. But it does mean if you get the honor of using your skills to be part of the economy, you are blessed.

Freedom. As Americans, it is a tremendous privilege to have the freedom we have in speech, religion, and a variety of other areas. Many men and women have given their lives to gain our freedom and protect it. We should never take it for granted.

Faith. As a person of faith, I believe God has given me tremendous privilege. The ability to know Him, recognize His presence, feel His love, and respond to His call is a tremendous gift.

Life. Our next breath is not guaranteed. If we experience it, we're fortunate. While life is full of sorrow and struggles, everyone alive should feel gratitude for having been given another day.

In every circumstance we should find the privilege in the moment. It doesn't mean we live in denial. It doesn't mean we ignore the sorrow. But it does mean that in the midst of the struggle we find reasons to give thanks. We find the privilege and with it comes a different perspective.

Thank you for reading.

Notes

Made in the USA
Columbia, SC
15 September 2017